Hallelujah!

98 Ways to Get From Where You Are To Where You Want to Be!

By Joe Stumpf

Hallelujah!
98 Ways to Get From Where You Are To Where You Want to Be!
By Joe Stumpf
Copyright ©2014 by Joe Stumpf
All rights reserved. First edition 2014

Published by By Referral Only, Inc.
2035 Corte Del Nogal, Suite 200
Carlsbad, CA 92011
www.byreferralonly.com

Contents

Introduction

Hi. I am Joe Stumpf, founder of By Referral Only.

For me, writing a book like this is like playing on a playground.

Here I get to share, create, and teach whatever I want that will help *you* get from where ever you are right now to where you want to be.

Since 1981 I have been writing my thoughts, concepts, insights and awareness into my journals.

I have 7,305 pages of *stuff*, all kinds of stuff that I have observed in my lifetime. I have had unprecedented access to the most successful people in all of North America.

I have observed and journalized exactly what they do, what they don't do, how they think, and how they out-wit, out-maneuver, and out-fox virtually everyone.

I have read over 2,000 books on personal development, business success, spiritual awareness, health, nutrition, relationships, leadership, and management.

I have interviewed and met with hundreds of authors who are experts in a wide variety of disciplines. Everything I have experienced has been captured in my journals.

I have a rich and active – sometimes overly active – mind and imagination. When I doubted myself and my value to the world, my writings reminded me that I am a keen observer, a smart and thoughtful loving man who simply loves to teach everything he learns.

During the past 30 years, I have invested hundreds of hours in personal development workshops, therapy and self-reflection.

I have emerged from that experienced a much wiser, compassionate, and generous man, **hallelujah!**

From the writings of Paramahansa Yogananda, I have come to deeply enjoy and relish my solitude and slowly comprehend the meaning of his words: Seclusion is the price of greatness.

My ideal day begins and ends in quiet reflective time.

I begin my day with a 30-minute ritual of writing about my intentions for the day. I believe that my intentions determine what gets my attention.

My Morning Questions

I use these three questions every morning to help me create and focus my intentions:

1. Imagine the day is over - What one thing would I like to achieve by the time I go to bed tonight that will give me the greatest sense of progress?

2. What can I do today to move in the direction of a higher version of myself?

3. How can I improve the well being of each person I plan to see today?

I have come to love the morning silence, knowing that God sits with me. I concentrate on joyful incidents. I dwell on all the joy in my life. I visualize what will give me the feelings I desire – the feeling of joy and freedom and growth. I end my ideal day with 30 minutes of reflection.

This thirty-minute period of time before I sleep allows me to complete my day by mentally creating the space for a deep, peaceful sleep. I choose daily to let go of worries and enter into this absolute silence.

My Night Time Questions

I write about my day using these three questions to prompt my writing:

1. What did I experience today?

2. What did I learn from my experiences?

3. Knowing what I know now, what would I do differently?

Journaling my journey daily – based on the people I meet, the books I read, the tapes I listen to, the places I visit, and the experience I am enjoying – is my path to peace.

What you can expect from this book are 98 of my best excerpts from my past journals, from my current thinking that is going into my everyday journals, and from my latest findings about building a great life.

Hallelujah!

Joe Stumpf

#1 The Message of a Master

The Message of a Master, by John McDonald: A classic tale of wealth, wisdom and the secret of success.

I love this book. It's on my wisdom bookshelf.

First published in 1929, this 83-page gem is the one of the first books to use the short story formula that I have come to call the "Blanchard Formula."

Ken Blanchard, the co-author of the *One-Minute Manager* and about fifteen other 100-page books, uses a simple formula to teach profound principals.

John McDonald uses the story of the executive in search of the truth about success. Here are some passages that really resonate with my way of thinking:

Open To Learning New Ways

"Those who think they know everything will learn nothing.

"Those who approach a subject with doubt and resistance will learn very little.

"But those who take up any subject with an open mind, willing to learn anything that will contribute to their advancement, comfort, and happiness are wise."

First Doing the Interior Work

"Your mind can be likened to a house that has been cluttered over the years with thousands of unnecessary pieces of furniture, pictures, ornaments and other things, all strewn around and piled everywhere.

"The results are that, although the outside of the house may present a good appearance, the inside is a mess of confusion and disorder.

"It is impossible to accomplish anything under such conditions, for you cannot go after one thing without stumbling over another.

"There is no order. No purpose. No progress.

"The first necessary thing to do, then, is to rid that house of all the furnishings that are not essential to your success."

Power Question

What is one thing you will get rid of today that is cluttering your life, that's not essential to your success?

#2 How to Create Conscious Referable Behavior

First, what is consciousness?

Webster says consciousness is *awareness, sensitivity, and the ability to perceive the relationship between oneself and one's environment.* We use our conscious mind when we are thinking logically or carefully. Your referrability resides inside your conscious referable behavior.

Here are 10 quick thoughts that come to mind that are referable behaviors. Over the past 30 years, I have compiled a list of over 1,000 ways to improve your referrability. Check out these 10:

1. Tell the truth, no matter what!

2. Be on time!

3. Make no assumptions and always ask the question behind the question: What is important about _____ to you?

4. Check your thinking with my "Truth Serum Script."

5. Be more interested than interesting.

6. Acknowledge people frequently with notes.

7. Quickly admit when you're wrong.

8. Say "please" and "thank you."

9. Give people permission to share how they feel about your service. Be hungry for feedback.

10. Speak with confidence and passion, do your homework and never wing it. If you don't know the answer, say so.

I was doing some private coaching for a real estate consultant and I had to point out to her that she talked for 45 minutes straight without asking me one question.

I brought into her consciousness that referable relationships have equal amounts of give and take.

It was painful for her at first to recognize this; however, after 15 minutes of playing "The Question Game," she became aware of how unskilled she was at being interested. She was unconscious to the fact that she wanted to be interesting more then she wanted to be interested.

So, look at the list of ten behaviors. Which ones can you bring into conscious constructive behavior?

Rain falls as a result of a change in the temperature. So in a like manner, a change in your referrability happens as a result of a change in your state of consciousness.

You must develop a referrability consciousness.

Go For It!

#3 Three Conscious Money Commitments

Here are a few commitments that I've made at a very conscious level to change my relationship with money. First, I committed to having a good time in my relationship with money. I have fun with money. Money is fun for me.

I'm committed to healing my relationship with money. I'm committed to clearing up anything in the way of my ability to have a healthy relationship with money.

I'm committed to *owning* my complete development as a financially independent individual. I have no entitlements; nobody owes anything to me when it comes to money. I'm committed to reinventing myself constantly in my relationship with money and not concealing myself.

I'm *committed* to full financial empowerment of people around me. And I'm committed to acting out of the awareness that I'm 100% responsible for, and the source of, my current financial state. I love my current financial state. I love where I'm at.

Through these commitments I've created a whole new set of beliefs that helped me, and continue to help me, improve my relationship with money.

What is your relationship with money?

What's your commitment to your relationship with money?

What are you committed to?

#4 How to Never Be Wounded by Normalcy

Once a friend said something to me that haunted me through the rest of the night.

He said, "Joe, I describe myself as a man who is wounded by normalcy."

Wounded by normalcy. I thought, "Wounded by normalcy." I started thinking, "What is normal?" Really – What is "normal"?

Normal, in many ways, is just kind conforming. Normal is pretty much the opposite of extraordinary, or it's the opposite of astonishing.

You would say, "That is not normal. It's extraordinary. That's astonishing." I thought, "Wow. I used to be pretty normal." I would say that at one time "wounded by normalcy" applied to me.

What Would A "Normal" Person Do Now?

Over the years, I have noticed that I changed that. I changed it because I missed out so many exciting, and even astonishing, experiences because I had this belief system that what "normal" people in this situation would do. That was my filter. I would ask myself; "What would a 'normal' person do now?"

Then I started thinking about *you* and I wondered, are you skipping, or really jumping over, the excitement of picking an event in your life that would allow you to get out of your comfort zone and *really* challenge yourself, something that you would not normally do?

Or are you getting stuck?

Or are you wounded by normalcy because it's not what you do "normally"?

I was wondering. I just wonder what you want to be.

Do you want to be "normal"?

 Or maybe you just want to be astonishing?

What do you want to create?

What might happen in your life if you took three or four months to prepare yourself to do something that really change something in your life?

I mean, *for life;* not just changed it *in* your life, but changed it *for* your life.

Sometimes the greatest risk of all is not taking a risk, especially when it comes to doing something that might change your life when it's time to do something *really astonishing.*

Imagine, just imagine for a moment, that the purpose of your life is to create a personal development plan that represents a version of yourself that you would describe as astonishing. Just imagine that.

#5 Avoid at All Cost Doing Things – or Not Doing Things – that You Will Regret Forever

Avoid at *all* cost doing things – or *not* doing things – that you will *regret* forever. The worst regrets are those things that you can't go back and fix. Avoid those regrets whenever you can. It's a huge principle to live on from this day forward. I mean it. Really avoid them because they can *haunt* you as time goes on and you never get a chance to go back.

Experience shows not many things will make a person more depressed – or more difficult to be around – than carrying a load of regrets for the things that were done, or the things that were not done, and it has become too late to do anything about them.

Time; it only works in one direction. That's what personal development is about. It's moving in one direction. Only our only our memories can take us back.

The time for action, the time to do something astonishing, is always in the present moment. Then you get to remember it for the rest of your life. That's a beautiful thing about doing astonishing things.

Replace Regrets with Astonishing Memories

There are things in our life that we have created in ourself that we don't want to remember. For example, choosing to hold a grudge. It's a choice; you're holding a grudge, or you're not forgiving or reconciling with someone. Is there anyone right now that, God forbid, if they died right now and you didn't have a chance to forgive them, or let it go, or complete with them. Imagine that happened. Then you had to carry it around, unfinished guilt or grief, and carry that resentment for the rest of your life.

You know what might be astonishing for some of you right now is to forgive or to let go – to go back and make amends to a person before they die; before you die. Really, is there an opportunity for you to do that? To clean up something in the past so you can move forward free of that? That's personal development.

You're not taking advantage of opportunities to tell the truth. Is there any area of your life right now that you may have not taken the advantage of telling the truth? You'd regret it forever if something happened and you didn't get a chance to tell the truth.

Is there something that you're doing that you're choosing not to spend time with the people who really are loving you when you're loving them? I mean, would you regret that if you were to leave right now, or they were to leave this place, and you could have spent more time with them? Right now, could you go back and say, "I'm going to spend time with them so I would never regret that?

Or is there somebody that you have not thanked completely? I mean really, fully acknowledged them in a personal communication or a really well-written communication.

Or is there someone that you haven't apologized to and really completed with them, and really let them know exactly how you feel? These are the things that can make our lives *so* much richer when we do them *before*; before the opportunity passes.

The Time to Learn Is When the Lesson Is Being Delivered To Me

I've lived my life very focused, and largely since I got sober in 1984, avoiding regrets by seizing the moment. Yet, like everybody, I've got regrets. There are things I've done in the past, even the past five/six years, I really regretted. I have this regret that I quit guitar lessons with my daughter, Olivia. I really missed a great chance to learn the guitar with her. Even though I would love her to have this musical skill in her life, and something that we could share together, I know that Olivia's life would be much more dimensional if I would have stuck with it several years when we were taking lessons.

The lessons were right in front of us. We were being taught. The teacher was there. We were meeting at my house, and we were meeting every Thursday. Then something happened where we missed a couple. Then we missed the next one, and we missed the next one. Then it was time to renew and I didn't renew.

I regret it. I don't feel guilty like I did something wrong, but I regret it; I have a healthy regret. I've learned something really important from that.

What I'm learning right now is the time to learn it is when the lesson is being delivered to me.

I choose to live a life, from this moment forward, regret-free. 'Cause time flows only in one direction.

#6 How to Develop an Attitude of Gratitude

I imagine you like me love to feel successful, but did you know that gratitude is the success turbo-charger?

I don't have to tell you again that what you focus on increases.

What I would love to suggest is when you feel grateful for what you have, you *focus on the good in your life* and it increases.

Feel grateful for your business circumstances, whatever they are, and they will start to improve.

This is a great antidote if you ever find yourself worrying, and often leads to positive action.

You can *make a list right now* of the people, experiences and things you're grateful for, then review it regularly. If you want to really accelerate your wealth, imagine yourself already having it, then feel grateful for the wealth you're going to have!

Research revealed that the happiest people were the ones who focused on how grateful they were with where they're at, and the unhappy but financially successful people were focused on what they *didn't* have and how far they had to go to get where they wanted to be next.

It would be nice to happy and successful, wouldn't it?

#7 How to Choose to Be Happy Now

People think, "I'll be happen when…" but our minds like what is familiar.

So if you want to be happy when you're generating leads, setting up appointments, writing contracts, completing transactions, and getting referrals, practice being happy *now!*

Laugh, celebrate your achievements, share your success with your friends and family, be excited about every victory you have, big or small – you celebrate them all.

Experience shows that when you commit to being happy *now,* the journey of building your business systems becomes much more enjoyable.

You might even like to imagine how you'll feel when 50% of your clients are referring you during the transaction, and you're generating a 20% yield on the relationships you have created in your After Unit.

Then start feeling that *now.* It doesn't cost any extra to feel like you have achieved your goals before you've achieved them.

A great question to ask is, "What else can I do to increase my happiness today and into the future?"

#8 How to Convert Your Courage to Confidence

A friend of mine told me that when you do the right thing, no matter what, the courage you use gets converted to confidence.

As you know, courage isn't acting without fear; it's acting *despite* fear.

You get the confidence after you do the right thing.

Make a list of all the things you want to get accomplished in your business that you are avoiding because you thought you lacked the confidence.

Do you want more leads, more appointments, more contracts, more closings and referrals?

Are you willing to start doing one thing at a time that is on your list?

I promise you that by the time you've done less than half the things on your list, your confidence will be humongous.

The question to ask today is, how can I use my courage to build my confidence going forward?

Today make it a confident day!

#9 How to Turn Action into Results

As you take action, you turn your strategies into systems and systems into results.

Keep in mind that whatever your dream is for your business, action will help you move beyond fear and turn your dreams into reality.

My friend Milton says, "Action is the greatest teacher there is."

Action is the antidote for fear and anxiety, and the remedy for indecisiveness.

Write down all the things you've been worrying about, then ask, "What can I do to make progress on this?"

"What can I do today to start creating the future I deeply desire?"

The question to ask yourself today is, "What can I do right now and going forward that will have the biggest impact on the results in my business?"

Make it an action day.

#10 How You'll Feel When You're Getting All the Referrals You Want

People move towards what they think about, and one of the most powerful ways to guide your thoughts is to feel how you'll feel when you've got what you want.

Stop for a moment and allow yourself to imagine yourself enjoying the effect of all the referred business that is coming your way that you created because you have strong and effective Before, During and After systems.

As you begin to imagine yourself enjoying the rewards of having a BY REFERRAL ONLY business that you've created, notice what you see and what you hear.

And as you allow yourself to do this, feel how you'll feel when you experience this new level of accomplishment.

People like what is familiar, and as you start becoming more familiar with feeling like you have already fully systematized your BY REFERRAL ONLY business, you will unconsciously begin to take steps to bring that deliberate, organized business system into realty for yourself. How does it feel to have a deliberate, organized business system?

Feel your way today!

#11 How to Courageously Question Your Limiting Beliefs

I believe that my beliefs do shape my reality and my results. I imagine my limiting beliefs create my limited results.

I'm actively discovering my limiting beliefs with simple sentence completion exercises.

Gosh, I enjoy writing the words, "asking for referrals is", several times on a piece of paper and then I complete the sentence with whatever thought comes to my mind. I'm discovering that I believe that asking for referrals is a way to convert my courage to confidence.

I love that thought. I love the thought that I'm asking for referrals courageously because I am confident that my deliberate organized business systems will support every client.

I am really referable.

I am becoming more and more aware of opportunities, resources and people that will help me to move towards my goal.

I have decided to really enjoy the process because it doesn't cost me any extra to be referable. I love asking myself each day, "What will I do to continuously develop my referrability?"

I love the thought that Joe Stumpf and By Referral Only are on your team to help you get from where you are to where you want to be.

#12 How to Delay Hesitation and Procrastination

It seems like hesitation and procrastination attack us in different ways.

It might sound or look like this: "What's the use – it doesn't matter anyway" or, "It doesn't make a difference when I do it" or, "I can't see myself doing that" or my all-time favorite, "I'll do it tomorrow."

Notice that when a person hesitates, they procrastinate, and they halt progress and miss out on all the things they would be learning by taking action.

If you have to put something off, I suggest you delay hesitation and procrastination!

 Whenever you feel the urge to hesitate and then procrastinate, take action towards your goal immediately.

Soon you'll have replaced the hesitation/procrastination habit with a positive action habit, and the rewards you'll discover in terms of energy are humongous.

So today ask yourself, "What business-building, lead-generating, referral-getting strategy have I been putting off that I can take action on today?"

Take action today!

#13 How to Get Comfortable Being Uncomfortable

What you did in your business yesterday is the "Old World." It worked well enough to keep you in business. Until today, which is the "New World."

When you've been doing something for a while, whether it's not asking for referrals, or working without clear boundaries, or not staying in frequent communication with friends, family and past clients, it's typically smooth sailing until you start to change.

You come to THE MAIN EVENT Master or BROVANCE and you see, hear, and feel how Before, During and After strategies have greatly impacted the businesses of thousands of agents and lenders worldwide.

You now decide to do something different. Then your mind sets off the alarm bells, and you may feel like hesitating or procrastinating.

Experience has proven that whenever you meet resistance to a new idea – that is a good sign.

This is a signal that *you're moving out of your comfort zone.* It's time to celebrate!

Pat yourself on the back! You're really making changes and you've got evidence. *Now keep going!*

Be uncomfortable today.

#14 How to Be Laser-Specific

I've heard Zig Ziegler say that you are either a wandering generality or a meaningful specific.

I wonder – is it time for you to get laser-specific about what you want?

There's a big difference between saying, "I want more referrals" and saying, "I want 50% of the people who buy, sell or borrow with me to introduce a person to me who will also buy, sell or borrow within 60 days after our introduction."

Obviously one is very vague, the other is laser-specific.

Experience shows that what you focus on increases. If you focus on something vague, what shows up is vague.

It's like using a magnifying glass to burn a hole in paper; you need to get the light to a fine point, then focus it for long enough to make a difference.

How can you *get even more laser-specific about what you want* to create in your Before Unit, During Unit and After Unit?

Be specific today.

#15 How to Love Affirming Your Predictability, Consistency and Reliability

Do you want to feel good more often?

How about get more leads, set up more appointments, write more contracts, complete more transactions, get more referrals, or just be happier?

Experience shows that you can create consistent, predictable, reliable monthly income in your life, but first you need to become comfortable with the idea that you *deserve* to have predictable, consistent, reliable monthly income.

One way you can start conditioning your comfort zone for predictable, consistent, reliable, monthly income is to use specific affirmations.

Here is a super-powerful affirmation worth writing several times a day and reciting in the mirror every morning:

"I love the thought that I am enjoying a predictable, consistent, reliable monthly income of $_____."

Your predictable, consistent, reliable monthly income will come to you faster and faster as you get comfortable with being a consistent, predictable, and reliable person.

Affirm yourself today.

#16 There Is Nothing to Fear, Except Fear Itself

Don't tell anyone this – because I know this may come as a shock to you – but everything is going to be OK.

It's worth reminding yourself that you've managed to come through everything that's ever happened in your life.

Right now it's worth noticing that real estate markets come and go, sometimes they're up and sometimes they're down.

It's funny how some people choose to worry about things they have no control over, like the market. Experience shows that fears, worries and anxieties only come when a person imagines unpleasant things in the past or the future.

When you allow yourself to get present, you'll realize that all is well right now.

As Roosevelt said, there is nothing to fear, except fear itself.

Today you feel the fear and do it anyway.

#17 How to Make a Decision to Be Referable

One of the simplest, most powerful things you can do to positively influence your increasing referrability is this:

Make a decision to be referable.

Once you've begun taking action, you'll start becoming aware of opportunities, resources, and people who will help you move towards your goal.

And having made this decision, you may as well decide to really enjoy the process.

After all, it doesn't cost any extra to be referable.

Having made the decision to be referable, what will you do today to develop your increasing referrability?

Today *decide* to be referable!

#18 You *Are* Free OF fear

I love reminding myself that I have managed to come through everything that has ever happened in my life.

Right now it's worth noticing that the real estate markets come and they go. Sometimes they're up and sometimes they're down.

It's funny how some people choose to worry about things that they have no control over, like the market.

Experience shows that fears, worries, and anxieties only come when a person imagines unpleasant things in the past or in the future.

When I allow myself to get present, I realize that all is well right now.

#19 How To Get What You Expect

Experience shows that the most successful, fulfilled and happy BY REFERRAL ONLY members have an extremely referable view of themselves.

Whatever the situation, they tell themselves, "I'm worthy of referrals."

Here's how it works:

When you expect to be referred, things happen; your brain starts to find evidence to prove you're referable.

It's even easier to develop a referable outlook than you might expect.

Say to yourself, "I am referable," and then start allowing yourself to notice the opportunities everywhere when you can ask for a great referral.

Today ask yourself this empowering question:

"What good things can I notice right now about this situation that would make it easy and fun for me to ask for a referral?"

Today get what you expect!

#20 How Big Can You Think?

Have you ever met a person who was focused on avoiding failure?

I'm not going to tell you the most successful, fulfilled and happy people focus on what's possible because they do more than that – **they also think BIG!**

When you *think big* and set goals that really excite and inspire you, you *release your creative powers* to help you achieve them.

When you focus in what you want (even if you don't know how you're going to do it), you'll begin to discover ways to bring your dreams into reality.

If you could wave a magic wand and create the deliberate, organized business system you desire, what would you see, hear and feel?

And what happens when you imagine deciding that you'll *do whatever it takes* to bring this about?

Today ask yourself several times, "What would I do if I knew I could not fail?"

Today think big!

#21 Everything Is a Cinch by the Inch and Hard By the Yard

I can remember the day I read *Think and Grow Rich* for the first time.

I learned that you can have whatever you want.

I immediately started setting several big, harry, humongous goals.

Then one day my coach said, "Everything is cinch by the inch."

He suggested, "Why don't you practice with one goal at a time and it will be a bit more achievable?"

I relaxed because it seemed easier.

We like what's familiar so much so that sometimes we become comfortable with *not* getting things done because we are trying to do so much at one time.

Here's a good idea: **Use familiarity in your favor.**

Get comfortable with some small successes, and the bigger ones will follow.

Today it's a cinch by the inch.

#22 What *Now* Time Is It?

Thomas Leonard said, "If you want a fantastic future, then focus on making the present precious."

I love that thought.

Remember something in the past. Now, notice it's just an idea in our minds called *memory.*

Think about something that might occur in the future.

Notice all this is happening *now*. You're thinking about the past and the future right now. Imagine a clock and every hour has the words NOW.

So, what time is it now? It's *now.*

The present is all that really exists, but that's OK, because that's always where you are.

Stop for a minute and allow yourself to get in touch with this moment. Whenever you've accomplished anything, it's in the present.

All of your moments of tremendous insight have also taken place in the present.

As you think of all the experiences of great pleasure and happiness you've had in your life, when they happened, it was *now.* Your mind and body always think it's *now,* so it's a good idea to get used to enjoying your present...*now!*

#23 How to Start Feeling Like You Have It

When you concentrate too much on wanting – "I want leads" or, "I want appointments" or, "I want contracts" or, "I want closings" or, "I want referrals" – it presupposes that you don't have it, and sends the message to your unconscious that you are lacking in some way.

Be careful that you don't become familiar with the feeling of *wanting.*

If that happens, the mind stops us having what we want, so we can continue having the familiar feeling of *wanting.*

Or even worse; we get what we want, and find it to be unsatisfying, returning us to the familiar feeling of *wanting.*

An alternative is to feel how you'll feel when you *have* a steady stream of leads, that are converting to Five-Star appointments, that easily sign contracts, and effortlessly close, and generously introduce you.

You'll let go of the feeling of *wanting,* and become familiar with the feeling of *having.*

Today feel like you already *have* it.

#24 If You Can Feel What You Want, You Can Have It

What happens when you feel like you have a predictable, consistent, reliable income?

What happens when you feel like your business is being run by deliberate, organized systems?

You know you want a predictable, consistent, reliable income being produced by a deliberate, organized business so **you can have** whatever you want.

How do I know?

Because people don't want *things* so much as the *feelings* those things will give them.

And you already have those feelings inside you. The great thing is, the more **you practice** feeling the feelings of already having a predictable, consistent, reliable income created by an organized, deliberate business system, the more will be attracted toward you like a magnet everything and everyone who will give you your predictable, consistent, reliable income.

Don't **believe me**? Let me ask you this: What feelings have you been feeling over the past months and years about your income and your business systems? And what has been attracted into your life?

See what I mean? Feel how you'll feel when you've got what you want, and you'll really begin to realize you can have whatever you want.

#25 You Drift in the Direction of the People You Hang Out With

My friend John Assraf says that you can make a list of your top five friends' annual income and divide it by five, and it will be darn close to yours.

I don't know if that is true or not, but I do know people are natural imitators; we tend to imitate the people we spend time with, adopting their beliefs, attitudes and behaviors.

If you spend a lot of time with people who have negative attitudes, a scarcity mentality, or destructive behaviors, the prognosis is poor.

But as you continue finding ways to spend more and more time with people who are positive, motivated, and committed to deliberate and organized business systems that produce consistent, predictable, reliable income, you'll love the outcome.

To supercharge your results, you might like to create a group of like-minded people who meet each week to explore referral lead-generating ideas and support each other in reaching their goals.

Notice people you want in your life?

Today hang with people who pull you up.

#26 What You Think about You Talk about, and What You Talk about You Bring about, So What Are You Thinking About?

Earl Nightingale says you become what you think about all day long.

If that's true, then it's safe to say your thoughts become your reality. If you're not sure what you've been thinking, have a look around!

What you focus on increases, so whatever's been showing up over time is what you've been focusing on.

Of course, your actions will give you clues about what you believe, too. If you've been thinking about consistent, predictable, reliable income, then more than likely you have an organized, deliberate business system. It's really great to know that your behavior is telling you what you've *really* been thinking.

And awareness is the first step in allowing you to choose a *new* thought. Focus on how you'll feel when you've got a predictable, consistent, reliable income. Think about what it will look like, sound like and feel like when you have a deliberate, organized Before, During and After system running your business.

All day today it's about being the highest version of you.

#27 You Find Proof for What You Think

My friend Jamie Smart says what the thinker thinks, the prover proves, because the human mind has two main functions: a thinker and a prover.

Whatever the thinker thinks, the prover proves that thought to be true.

If a person thinks about consistent, predictable, reliable monthly income, their prover will prove that to be true.

If they think about how abundant leads, appointments, contracts, closings, and referrals are, the prover will prove *that* to be true.

Over time, the circumstances of your business come into alignment with whatever you've been thinking.

Your current lead-generating results, your appointment conversion results, your contracts written, and your number of closings are the result of what you've been thinking and feeling over time.

Why not ask yourself what thoughts you'd like to have so you can prove that you do have the peace and pleasure that a consistent, predictable, reliable monthly income provides?

Today what the thinker thinks, the prover proves.

#28 How *Willing* Are You?

I was once told that my progress in business would be directly linked to my willingness to do whatever it takes to create organized, deliberate business systems.

When I first heard that, I had to look at how willing I really was to have a predictable, consistent, reliable monthly income.

What you may discover over time is just how powerful willingness really is. It seems to me that when you become willing to do whatever it takes, you really begin to unlock the power of your unconscious mind.

Once you've created your vision of a deliberate, organized business system producing a predictable, consistent, reliable monthly income, say to yourself, "I am willing to do whatever it takes to create the peace and happiness that a consistent, predictable, reliable income will provide me."

Then notice and accept the thoughts and feelings that come up. If you don't feel willing yet, ask yourself, "Am I willing to become willing?"

A useful tool is to ask, "What is my current level of willingness, on a scale of one to 10, and am I willing for it to go higher?" As you start to become aware of your developing willingness, you'll begin to notice that it is easier than you think to create an organized business system. Today ask yourself, "Am I willing to do whatever it takes to be happy, joyful and free?"

#29 *Carpe Diem*...Seize the Day

My favorite teacher said to me, "Don't be fooled by the calendar. There are only as many days in the year as you make use of."

Stop for a moment, take a couple of deep breathes, and realize that as you listen to me you are occupying a unique space, at a time in history that will never be repeated.

Some people lose their day to others, by perceiving themselves as victims: "I hate working with these clients!" or, "I can't believe they are shopping rates on me!" or, "My manager doesn't understand me."

But you can realize that these are *choices.* You don't *have to* do anything. If there's something that you've been thinking that you *had* to do, you can restate it as, "I *choose* to find a way to keep this transaction together with these clients" or, "I *choose* to let these clients work with a different consultant" or, "I *choose* to find away to finance my client's dreams" or, "I *choose* to seek to understand what my manager wants and not work so hard trying to get *him* to understand *me.*"

It's your choice, and it always has been. Don't let anyone or anything take your day. Seize this day and own it all.

Today seize the day!

#30 How to Imagine Your Perfect Day

I wonder what happens when you imagine your perfect day?

Imagine there is a miracle in the night, and when you wake up tomorrow, everything was exactly as you'd like it to be:

You have an organized **Before Unit** getting a $15-to-$1 return on your marketing dollars, a **During Unit** generating a 50% referral rate, and an **After Unit** yielding a 20% return.

And you're doing all this in a reasonable amount of time. Imagine that.

What would you see, hear, feel, and believe that would let you know the miracle had taken place? Walk through your perfect day in your mind's eye feeling the impact of a deliberate, organized business system running your business.

Where are you? Who's with you? How are you spending your time? What's your financial situation?

How motivated do you feel as you begin to consider the things you would do with your time?

Ask yourself now, "How can I continue bringing my perfect day even closer today?"

Today *see* your perfect day.

#31 A Setback Is a Setup for a Comeback

Everyone who has created a deliberate, organized business system has experienced setbacks along the way.

Mary Kay says a setback is a setup for a comeback.

I love that thought.

Most people give up when they meet setbacks and obstacles, but because you choose to be successful, you do what you did when you learned to walk.

When you fall over, learn from the experience, pick yourself up and keep going!

Oprah says you do what you do when you know what you know; when you know different, you do different.

It may take some time to create the predictable, consistent, reliable flow of monthly income you desire, but when you *stay true to yourself* and keep learning, you develop wisdom and insight.

You might even decide to eliminate "failure" from your vocabulary!

A fabulous question to keep in mind all day today is, "How can I enjoy learning from the setbacks I've experienced?"

#32 How to Let Go of Trying

Try to stand up or try to sit down.

Notice what happens when you *try* anything – it means you do nothing.

Try to have consistent, predictable, reliable income.

When people say they're going to *try,* they're planning to *fail.* Notice if you have been trying for years to make various changes.

Now notice if the feeling of *trying* has become familiar.

People like what's familiar, so once you get used to *trying,* the mind doesn't want to shock you by letting you succeed!

Have you become familiar with the experience of trying or struggling?

If so, it may be time to find out what happens when you *move beyond trying.*

What happens when you *imagine having the magic words to get referrals memorized?* How does it feel?

Start feeling successful, and focus on having what you want now. As the famous philosopher Yoda said, "Do or do not – there is no *try.* "

Today let go of *trying.*

#33 When You're Persistent, You Get Predictable

It seems to me that persistent people begin their success where others end in failure.

Every business-building journey has obstacles.

But as you build systems that generate low-cost, high-quality leads that convert to good, solid appointments with Five-Star prospects, and keep moving forward to write contracts, complete transactions, and generate referral leads, you increase and expand your personal power.

I've heard it said in many different ways that mistakes are learning opportunities, and failures contain the seeds of success.

When you stay committed to your vision and keep going despite obstacles and setbacks, you send a powerful message to your unconscious mind:

I deserve a consistent, predictable, reliable income and I'm willing to do whatever it takes to get it.

The more enthusiastic we are, the more productive we become. The more outgoing we are, the more helpful we become. The more persistent we are, the more predictable our success becomes.

Today be like a postage stamp and stick to it until you get there.

#34 How Today's Actions Become Tomorrow's Habits

People like the security of the familiar.

Today's actions are tomorrow's habits.

If you want to create a future that is different from the past, it's important you start getting familiar with that future.

If you want to be a wealthy person tomorrow, it's time to start thinking, feeling and acting like a wealthy person today.

What are the habits of the wealthy?

The key to creating those habits is to take action. Is what you're practicing today about where you've been or where you want to be?

What wealth habits can I start practicing today and in the days and the weeks ahead?

Today notice what wealth habits look like, what wealth habits feel like, and what wealth habits sound like.

#35 Focus on Creating Value for Others and the Money Will Follow

"How can I create a consistent, predictable, reliable income of $15,000 a month?"

"How can I consistently, predictably and reliably create $15,000 a month of value for all my buyers, sellers and borrowers?"

Money is an inevitable by-product when you give your creative gifts to the world.

What you focus on increases, so as you focus more on your *human life value,* you will begin to discover even more opportunities to take action.

At the same time, as you become even more focused on creating value, you'll start to discover that you're acting more and more from an abundant, creative mindset.

I have modeled my life on finding ways to give more value than anyone would expect and, as my friend Jesse says, that is very attractive.

Here is a good question: "How many ways can I create to give my human life value to other people?"

Today you focus on *value.*

#36 Focus on the *What* and the *Why*, and BY REFERRAL ONLY Will Take Care of the *How*

Victor Frankel said when you have a strong enough *what* and *why,* you can endure any *how.*

I love that thought. It means when you focus (thought plus emotion) on *what* you want, and *why* you want it, you activate the power of your unconscious mind.

That's when the *how* starts showing up, often without your even having to figure it out.

This is not to say you won't be required to do anything, but you can relax, let go of results, and trust your intuitive impulses about what to do.

That's the power of BY REFERRAL ONLY; we take care of most of the *how* for you, which is really amazing.

Long-time member Terry Moerler says to get motivated, just focus on the *what* you want and the *why* you want it, and BY REFERRAL ONLY will show you exactly *how* to get it.

Today you let go of the *how* and focus on *what* you want and *why* you want it.

#37 How to Get the Abundance Mindset

To create something exceptional, your mindset must be relentlessly focused on abundance. The scarcity mindset doesn't think there's enough business to go around.

The abundance mindset says, "There are plenty of people who want to buy, sell or borrow, flowing in the world, and more are coming into the market every day."

Successful BY REFERRAL ONLY consultants believe in abundance. Stop for a moment. Feel the air going in and out of your lungs.

Air is created by plants and trees, and flows around the world.

As you take each breath, you're not stopping the flow; you're joining it.

It's the same with the opportunity to help people who want to buy, sell and borrow. I suggest you become part of the flow.

Today ask yourself, "What evidence can I find today to support my developing abundance mindset?"

Today you breathe deeply while you embrace the abundance mindset now.

#38 How to Get Past the Fear of Asking for Referrals

Everyone wants to be accepted, don't you?

That's at the core for all of us: I want you to accept me. I want you to like me. I don't want you to reject me. An easy way to get people to accept you and not reject you is to avoid asking for anything.

That's the little child in us, that 10-year-old who learned early that you risk rejection when you put yourself in the position of asking someone for something.

So, you've got to recognize that that child has grown up. This is an adult in business. When you ask for a referral and the person says they don't know anyone, they're not saying they don't know anyone forever.

They're saying, "I don't know anyone right now." It's not a personal attack or a rejection.

Focus on gaining your acceptance from yourself, not from others.

Self-esteem is a lot of little victories over a long period of time that you add to an internal bank account.

Eventually you'll take bigger risks because you've got an account to withdraw from. The thing that kills self-esteem the fastest is setting unrealistic goals.

Don't get attached to the outcome; get attached to changing your behavior of asking.

#39 How to Learn From the Flower Lady

I was having dinner with a friend of mine at a nice downtown San Diego restaurant, when a lady selling flowers walked up to us and said, "Do you want to buy a flower for your lady?"

I would call that a "hard question," because it caused me to make a hard quick decision.

So I looked at the young lady and said, "Are you open for some coaching?" She enthusiastically said, "Yes, tell me."

I said, "I'm not going to tell you that your approach to selling flowers could be greatly improved because you already know that. What I would like to suggest is that you change your opening statement using my Magic Words Technology."

She smiled and said, "What is Magic Words Technology?"

I explained to her that her greatest opportunity to improve her ratio of flower sales is to use words that caused people to be five times more interested in what she is saying. I asked her out of ten people she approached now, how many would actually buy flowers?

She said one, maybe two.

I said, "I'm curious. Can you imagine what it would feel like if you had the exact words that caused four or five people out of ten to buy flowers from you?" She said, "That would be incredible!"

I asked, "I'm wondering, what's important about improving your flower sales by 100% to you?"

She said, "I could go home earlier and take care of my daughter." I said, "I won't tell you that you will feel better when you're home with your daughter instead of out here pumping flowers because you already know that, but I will tell you that until you change your approach you won't be home with your daughter."

She said, "What should I say?"

I felt the shift from me giving her advice to her asking me for help. This is a critical step if you want to influence people.

So I suggested that she use the following Magic Words when she approached a man to buy flowers for his lady.

I was wondering if you can imagine how happy you would feel by giving a beautiful flower to your lady.

The flower lady went into a trance. She said, "Say that again." So I took my pen out and wrote her script on the napkin.

I was wondering if you can imagine how happy you would feel by giving a beautiful flower to your lady.

I asked her to role-play it with me a few times to get the right tone and cadence.

She was really a terrific student.

We practiced it a half dozen times then I said, "It's show time. Go get 'em."

My friend and I watched with amazement as she sold seven out of eleven tables flowers.

She came back to our table beaming with joy. She looked me right in the eyes and said, "I'm going home."

It was a magic moment because one more time I realized that the right words at the right time delivered with the right intention are magical.

Now the ironic thing was over the next hour, three more flower sellers approached us with the statement "Do you want to buy a flower?"

We chuckled and chose not to do any more coaching that night.

Reflection

As you reflect on this story, what insight or new awareness did you receive, and how will you use them in your life to better serve others?

#40 How to Be Comfortable Being Uncomfortable

I'm comfortable moving out of the old world and into the new world. I'm loving change.

I'm loving the thought that everything is changing and I am comfortable with change.

I am more comfortable today asking for referrals.

I am more comfortable today communicating my boundaries.

I am more comfortable today staying in frequent communication with friends and family and past clients.

I'm choosing to do something different. Experience has proven that whenever I'm uncomfortable with a new idea, that's a good sign.

I'm loving my discomfort because it means I'm moving out of my comfort zone into my new world.

#41 How the Best Characters Make No Excuses

When they fail, they admit it and move on. They get back up and do it right the next time.

They let their actions speak louder than their words. No excuses, just results.

The Best Characters dare to dream.

While others live the mundane and settle into a life they never bargained for, a rut, the Best Characters dream of a better life. And then they take the risks necessary to achieve their dreams.

Must you be the best at what you do?

Nothing really significant gets done in life until you find what you must do, not what you want to do, not what you need to do, not what you would like to do.

You get real inspired when you find the character inside you to do what you must do.

Take inventory on the above characteristics and then start moving to bring your life in line with the characteristics of the "Best."

A Few Helpful Character Building Affirmations

I love the thought that I do what must to be done, even when it's difficult.

I love the thought that I take responsibility for my choices, my actions and my consequences.

#42 How to Be a Superior Communicator

This is a skill that is learned, not something you're born with.

Here are ten **advanced communication skills** to learn.

1. You Know How People Hear You.

You are so fully responsible for how you are heard that you experience the responses and reactions that the person with whom you are communicating is experiencing. You do more than just speak well. You ask people to tell you what they heard you say, so you can make sure you are communicating clearly.

2. What You Say Fits Perfectly

You don't make points just to make points. Instead, you feel what the other person needs to hear right then and you intuitively phrase the perfect thing to say. You do more than just "speak your truth." To say that "it fits" means it is true, useful and timely.

3. Everything You Say Expands a Person's Awareness

When you respond or give advice, the advice you give speaks both to the client's current situation or problem, but also expands their awareness without overwhelming them. You do more than just give good advice.

4. You Have a Highly Flexible Style

You have access to the full range of communication styles, tones of voice, and can immediately move along the continuum in a way that serves the person you're communicating with. You do more than just "be" your personality. You can be a curious consultant, a pit bull negotiator and observant overseer of the transaction.

It is a skill that is learned, not something you're born with.

5. You're a Weaver

You can remember what a client has said 10 minutes ago and weave in the point you are making right now to include that, and to include what they said the last time you spoke with them.

6. You Don't Babble; You're Not Know as a Talker

You speak very little, but when you do, it makes so much sense. You do more than talk. You give profound, insightful advice and ask thought-provoking questions.

7. You Have a Special Style

You are warm and inclusive, but not effusive or loud. You are not flat or charged-up. You do more than speak clearly. You speak the truth.

8. You Can Listen and Speak at the Same Time

You are so able to immediately hear when the other person has heard what you're talking about, that you instantly stop speaking and get that they got it. You do more than complete a sentence.

9. You're Not Trying to Get Your Needs Met

You add to the space instead of consuming or displacing it. You do more than try to be special.

10. You're Not Driven to Talk or Help.

You naturally seek to understand far more than needing to advise. You do more than try to make a difference.

#43 How to Create Confidence

What does it mean to be confident? Have you ever lost your confidence?

I'm not going to tell you that I'm always confident, but I will suggest that my confidence is always highest when things around me are happening in a predictable manner.

Have you noticed when things lose their predictability and become more random and chaotic, your confidence wanes?

Which leads me to the conclusion that when you don't have predictability, you give birth to self-doubt.

The fastest way to create confidence is predictability.

So are you like me, do you believe that confidence is a by-product of predictability?

So here is how I create predictability in my life so my confidence stays high.

When I notice that my confidence is low, I like to ask this simple question:

What three things can I do in the next 90 days that would get me 50% closer to the achievement of my life priorities?

This one question gets me refocused on my strengths.

So, staying confident keeps things predictable.

#44 Get a New Level of Language Competency

Three distinctions on what an advanced consultant understands about the power of language:

1. Phrasing vs. Vocabulary

Vocabulary has to do with the number and quality of the words we use to communicate. Phrasing is the ability to communicate ideas and deeper concepts.

An example of a great phrase would be: "I will represent your money like it is mine, and when it comes to making you money or saving you money I'm like a pit bull."

2. How Well You Come Across vs. What You Are Saying

How well you come across is as important as what you are saying – your tone of voice, pace, authenticity, energy, style and attitude matter.

Many folks try to have better things to say, but until they work on how they come across, they are less likely to be listened to.

3. Experiencing vs. Listening to the Other Person

Listening is a fairly passive process. They talk, you listen.

There is a level beyond listening and it is called *experiencing* the other person.

When you feel or sense what they *are* saying, *not* saying and *what's going on* over *there*, over *here* and *in between*, then you're truly listening, because you are noticing and absorbing the entire interaction, not just the words.

4. Synthesizes vs. Mimics/Repeats

You know how some people speak in clichés or platitudes? Or that they say the same thing to everyone they chat with? They are called mimics or repeaters.

They learn a good phrase and they use it! Better to be prompted to say something based on whom you are talking with. Let them influence you and evoke a customized vs. a stock response.

5. Awareness vs. Ignorance

This is pretty obvious. But you'll need to understand if the person you're speaking with is someone who even knows what awareness is or is sensitive to their environment.

If not, then adapt how you communicate to fit them, because they likely won't hear your more sophisticated approach.

6. Full Communicator vs. Appropriate

It's important to say all that needs to be said, yet say it appropriately. This is quite different from saying only what's appropriate to say.

Again, say what there is to say and find an appropriate way to say it. Don't hide behind the "appropriateness curtain."

7. English vs. Jargon

English refers to using simple words to make your point.

Jargon refers to using special or sophisticated words to make your point. Keep your jargon for use between similarly trained colleagues and be sensitive enough to adapt the jargon to English when working with clients or the public.

8. Who vs. What

Consulting focuses on the *who* and the *what*. The "who" refers to the client's values, innermost wants, and the complete self.

The "what" refers to linear goals, should, and needs.

The typical salesperson works primarily on the *what* and so can the consultant, but only if the consultant comes from the *who* first.

9. Fully Respond vs. Partially Respond

When someone says something to you that rings true (whether you like it or not), take the time to really listen and discuss it.

Learn in that moment what there is to learn; don't just hear it, deflect it and figure you'll get it later.

Take the time to learn now.

10. Light vs. Significant

Do you come across light or heavy? Do things matter a LOT to you or do you have faith? Light speakers are listened to because what they are saying has little packaging or baggage.

#45 What Is Important about Money to You?

When you ask yourself, *What is important about money to me?* notice that your answer falls into two categories: goals and values. Goals are tangible. They are usually related to specific things or experiences and have a monetary value like buy a car or remodel my home.

Values are intangible, the things in life that you care about most.

They don't carry a big price tag like freedom and purpose and security and greater connection to God.

What you want when you're focusing on developing a money-making mindset is to focus on your values because they are significant.

If you get clear on your values, it will help you feel a sense of comfort and trust, and will help you make better decisions about your goals.

One of the most interesting things that you'll ever do is ask the people that you really admire and mentor, what is important about money to them, and discover their values, and then compare them to yours.

A wise man told me that when your values are clear, your decisions are easy. When you meet people who have the wealth and the happiness that you desire, discover the intangible drive behind their drive.

Then do your best to align yourself with people who have similar values.

#46 How to Use Your Brain for Processing and Not for Storage

Is it time for you to fully embrace the concept of journaling and once and for all begin using your brain for processing and not for storage because you will feel freer and more creative?

You can start by taking notes from these daily messages in your new journal and then during the day, you can use it to make notes relating to your increasing financial intelligence and your progress.

You can use it to ask yourself questions about your beliefs and your goals and your commitments. You may be surprised as you begin to notice just how quickly you become aware of your changing habits and attitudes and beliefs when you write them down. And as you see your wealth continuing to grow, you can look back and feel real good that you're continually making progress. You might even ask yourself, what can I write in my journal today that I'm going to feel good reading a year from now? People ask me, "How can you get so much done?" and the one thing I say is that I record just about every worthwhile thought in my journal.

Because I know that once that idea is out of my head and on paper, my mind now has space for a new thought. If I don't capture it on paper like a prisoner, then my mind is being used as a filing cabinet to hold onto that thought and if I've learned anything in my lifetime, I've learned that my mind is far better at processing than collecting and storing thoughts.

#47 How to Develop Your Increasing Willingness and Ability to Receive More Money

Once you cause your money problems to be more impersonal, life becomes much easier and more interesting.

When a money problem baffles you, simply say to yourself: *it's not about me. It's about my skill at solving this particular money problem.*

If I don't know how to solve it, it simply means that I now know which money-making skill I need to learn. A money-making mindset says I know I'm at my best when I'm using my brain. My ideal day is when my business gives me a complex money problem to solve. I love digging into a problem a little bit like a jigsaw puzzle.

The puzzle is *im*personal. Getting the skills to solve the puzzle is personal. Many people have negative personal ideas about wealth, and so they unconsciously avoid it. Now do you want to discover what your hidden beliefs are about money?

It's simple. Just finish the sentence, "Money is..." with as many ideas as you can in two minutes, and once you've explored your existing ideas, start replacing any thoughts that are no longer useful with positive, energizing statements.

Instead of thinking about your money problems right now, become more willing to receive wealth because you can tell yourself, I love being wealthy and I'm willing to receive all the good that comes to me, rather than accepting just any thought and feeling which arises.

#48 How to Be Laser-Specific about Life

I am laser-specific about what I choose to have in my life. *I'm choosing 50% of the people who buy, sell or borrow from me to introduce a person to me who will buy, sell or borrow within 60 days after our introduction.*

My experience shows that what I focus on increases. I'm like a magnifying glass.

I'm so focused.

I always make a difference. I'm asking myself now how will I continue to get even more laser specific about what I choose to create in my before, during, and after unit.

I am loving affirming my consistency, predictability, and reliability. I choose feeling good.

I'm choosing to get more leads, set up more appointments, write more contracts, close more transactions, get more referrals, and just be happier.

I'm creating consistent, predictable, reliable income in my life because I am becoming more and more comfortable with the idea that I deserve to have predictable, consistent, reliable monthly income. I love the thought that I'm enjoying a predictable, consistent, reliable monthly income.

My predictable, consistent, reliable monthly income is coming to me faster and faster as I get more and more comfortable being a consistent, predictable, and reliable person.

#49 How to Keep More Than You Spend

Hey, did you know that many people who earn huge salaries are actually in debt?

I'm sure you've discovered that when you've pulled people's credit reports in the past.

And that's because they spend more than they earn.

One of the keys to becoming wealthy is to earn more than you spend which means produce more than you consume, and as you reduce your spending and you increase your earnings, your net worth will increase more and more.

One of the great things about this is that as you start to find ways to attract even larger flows of money into your life, you can feel good that your increasing wealth will be staying with you for long enough that you can enjoy it.

The question you want to ask today is, *How can I reduce what I consume and increase what I produce?*

Today you spend less than you make.

I love that thought.

#50 How to Be Consistent, Predictable and Reliable

I am feeling like I have a predictable, consistent, reliable income. I'm feeling like my business is being run by a deliberate, organized system.

I'm enjoying the results of a predictable, consistent, reliable income because I'm operating a deliberate, organized business. I'm focused on the feeling of getting anything that I want when I want it.

I know that the more I practice the feeling of already having a predictable, consistent, reliable income being created by a deliberate, organized business system, the more I'm attracted towards it like a magnet.

I am feeling like I have.

I am feeling how I'll feel when I have a steady stream of leads that are converted to five-star appointments that easily sign contracts and effortlessly close and generously introduce me.

I let go of the feeling of wanting and I'm becoming more familiar with the feeling of having.

I love the feeling that I get from the thought that I focus on feeling what it's like when I have what I desire.

That just feels good to me.

#51 How to Be in Love with the Now

I think of all my experiences with great pleasure and happiness.

Every one of them that I've ever had in my entire life, I love the thought that is happening now.

My mind and my body always think it's now.

So I believe it's a good idea to get used to enjoying my present now.

Right now!

It's my best moment. I'm in love with the now.

I am living in the now, now.

I believe my fantastic future is my reality because I'm focused on making my present precious.

I love that thought. I love my memory and my ability to visualize the future and I choose to live in the moment.

I love imagining a clock and every hour has the word "now." So when I ask myself, "What time is it?" I automatically say to myself, "It's now."

I stop for a minute and I allow myself to get in touch with the moment.

Whenever I accomplish anything in its present, I'm always in the moment. All my moments of tremendous insight have always taken place in my present.

#52 Embrace Every Problem as a Way of Increasing Your financial Intelligence

I've noticed that when you resist a money problem, what happens next is you may slowly and unconsciously drift into financial abyss.

Financial resistance easily cultivates self-doubt which causes us to avoid positive influence and always leads to poor judgment.

Experience shows that by looking financial adversity squarely in the face, we grow stronger, more capable and more responsible.

Open your world to the books, recordings, websites, videos and games that can help you accelerate your financial learning.

As you begin to increase your financial intelligence, you'll start to see opportunities appearing that you just wouldn't have noticed before.

And the next time, when you choose to experience a money problem as a way to increase your financial intelligence, you will accelerate your growth.

I suggest that you master the money-making mindsets because you may be surprised at how easily and automatically you find yourself making better financial decisions and taking even more positive action.

As your financial intelligence increases, ask yourself, How can I really enjoy increasing my financial intelligence even more today?

#53 Ten Questions to Help You Describe Your Relationship with Money

Now, what is your relationship with money?

I'm going to help you describe your own relationship with money because only when you know what your current relationship is can you start to transform it.

All I want you to do is write down the word that best describes it. I'll give you an alternative choice. Choose which word resonates truer for you:

1. When it comes to money, I feel open or secretive.

2. When it comes to money, I feel focused or vague.

3. When it comes to money, I feel pragmatic or I feel wishful.

4. When it comes to money, I feel obsessive or I feel peaceful.

5. When it comes to money, I feel attentive or I feel confused.

6. When it comes to money, I feel disorganized or organized.

7. When it comes to money, I feel generous or I feel reckless.

8. When it comes to money, I feel on time or behind schedule.

9. When it comes to money, I feel neurotic or controlled.

10.   When it comes to money, I feel strategic or impulsive.

Now look at the words that you feel represent your relationship with money.

How do you feel about your selection of your words? Your answer is what your *relationship* with money is today.

#54 How to Make a Commitment to Being Wealthy

I've heard it said that the bigger the commitment you make, the bigger the obstacles and the more resistance you will face.

I've also heard it said that one of the simplest, most powerful things you can do to positively increase your wealth and your abundance mentality is make a commitment to be wealthy.

Staying committed to a goal is easy when you love what you do. I love the thought that a commitment is born out of a meaningful goal.

It seems that when you're excited about making money, you're progressively moving towards the realization of a meaningful money goal. The obstacles and difficulties become solvable problems.

The secret seems to be staying committed to your goals and staying flexible in your approach. Once you've begun taking action, you'll start becoming aware of opportunities, resources and people that will help you move towards your goal.

Having made this commitment to wealth, you may as well commit to really enjoying the process. After all, it doesn't cost any extra to enjoy it. In my experience, the people who make the most money always know where they want to go even when they have no idea how they're going to get there. They're simply committed to getting there.

Ask yourself today, how committed are you to your goal, and if you're willing to start to manifest now, even though you may not know how to get there? I'm wondering, having made the commitment to be wealthy, what will you do today to develop your increasing wealthy.

#55 How to Think Big!

I'm fully embracing the thought, "Everything is a cinch by the inch - so I think big!"

I practice achieving one big goal at a time.

I'm relaxed as I focus on one thing at a time because it's easier that way. I like what's familiar so much so that sometimes I can become comfortable with not getting things done because I may be trying to do too much at one time.

I love this idea. I'm using familiarity in my favor. I'm being comfortable with small and big successes and I know even bigger ones will follow.

Think big!

I'm not just focused on what's possible because I do more than that. I also think big.

I think big.

I set goals that really excite and inspire me. I release my creative powers to help me achieve them.

When I focus on what I want even if I don't know how I'm going to do it, I discover ways to get things done.

I love thinking big. I'm a big thinker.

I love the feeling that my big thoughts give me. I love the thought, "What would I do if I knew I would not fail?"

#56 How to Make Full-Heartedness Your Antidote for Exhaustion

Have you ever noticed how much energy you get when you're fully absorbed in a project, problem or activity? Conversely, have you ever noticed how fatigued you get when you are partially invested in an activity and your mind is not fully focused on one thing but wandering from one place to the next, getting more tired by the moment?

You've learned about how a musician loses herself in her music, how a painter becomes lone with the process of painting? In work, sports, conversation or hobby, you yourself have experienced the suspension of time, the freedom of complete absorption in the activity.

This is called flow, an experience that this is flow, an experience that is at once demanding and rewarding, and experience that demonstrates that this is one of the most enjoyable and valuable experiences a person can have. In my experience, complete absorption is not only the antidote to fatigue; it is also the secret to mindfulness.

Full-heartedness puts you in the present moment, completely absorbed in the moment, releasing you from distracting clutter so you can generate creativity, productivity, and energy that is undiluted. Attention is power and when you work in a state of full-heartedness, you bring in almost supernatural power to what you do. Ask yourself now, How fully invested are you in the total absorption of one project at one time?

#57 How to Be a Person Who Is Easy to Refer

I am willing to be a person who is easy to refer. I do the mental work for positive change because I choose to be even more referable every day.

My motto is I go green because asking for and getting referrals for my clients during the process of helping them reach their goals is only natural and I allow each person to refer me.

My business is unlimited because it's all about one person telling another person who tells another person.

This connection is unlimited, which makes my business unlimited.

I am confident.

I speak with referral confidence, which means I consult, negotiate, and organize with so much expertise that my clients happily and passionately introduce me to the people that they care about.

I relax and I enjoy my client relationships. I know that whenever it is revealed to me, it is the perfect moment because the advice I give is always focused on making my clients' dreams come true.

#58 How to Make the System the Solution, Not You

Why do eight out of ten people who get into the real estate business leave within five years? I promise you, it's not because they are making a consistent, predictable, reliable income.

No, it's just the opposite. It's because they are frustrated, aggravated, fed up with living with uncertainty of their future income. So what went wrong with all these people?

Well, the answer is quite simple. They didn't have a system to generate leads, convert the leads to appointments, turn the appointments into contracts, and the contracts into closings while during the entire time generating referrals.

Now what I am describing is an impersonal system. It's the same thing that Starbucks has. It's an automatic process and because of the automatic process, the people who've worked there can show up and be personal.

By Referral Only is a system for operating your real estate and your mortgage business. It's a **Before Unit system** that includes programs such as the Getting Listings.

It's the **During Unit system** which is the powerful initial consultation dialogues, the magic words that get referrals, the magic words that remove resistance.

It's the **After Unit system** that systematizes your touch points that nurture lifetime relationships and remind your past clients to introduce you to their family, friends and colleagues.

The system is the solution – not you, not me. So let's get busy installing these systems into your business so you can have consistent, predictable, reliable monthly income.

#59 How to Choose to Be Happy Now

People think "I'll be happy when ____." But our minds like what's familiar, so if you want to be happy when you're wealthy, practice being happy now.

The more you enjoy the process of becoming wealthy, the more you'll enjoy the result. Laugh, celebrate your achievements, share your success with friends and loved ones.

Experience shows that when you commit to being happy now, the journey to your increasing wealth becomes much more enjoyable.

You might even like to imagine how you'll feel when you're wealthy. Then start feeling that right now. It doesn't cost any extra to feel good. So what else can you do right now to increase your happiness today and into the future?

Because I am happy, I generate leads, set up appointments, write contracts, close transactions, and get referrals, all because I practice being happy now.

I'm enjoying the process of building my By Referral Only business systems because I love the feeling of the results that are on their way right now. I laugh and celebrate my achievements.

I am referable because I constantly ask, "How can I give more value which makes my client's experience of buying, selling, or borrowing full of joy?"

I'm in the joy business because I know that my future prosperity is directly connected to the value and the joy that I create for my buyers, my sellers, and my borrowers.

Yes, I imagine how I feel as I'm getting a great introduction to a five-star prospect from a client who loves sharing about their experience with everyone they love.

#60 How to Feel Your Results Now

I love the experience of committing myself to being happy now because the journey of building my business systems is so enjoyable, each day I choose to imagine how I feel getting 50% of my clients from the During unit and getting a 20% yield on my relationships I've created in my After unit.

I know it doesn't cost me anything extra to feel like I've achieved my goals, even before I've achieved them. And I love to ask myself, "What else can I do to increase my happiness today and into my future?"

I love the thought that I convert my courage to confidence.

I believe my courage isn't about acting without fear.

It's acting despite fear because I get my confidence after I do the right things.

I love the feeling of the thought of getting more leads, more appointments, more contracts, more closings, and more referrals, and I'm willing to start doing one thing at a time on my list because by the time that I've done half the things on my list, my confidence is soaring.

I love the question, "How can I use my courage to build my confidence going forward producing massive results?"

#61 How to Increase What You Want More Of

Whatever you focus your attention on increases over time.

People turn small credit card debt into large credit card debt by focusing on the credit card debt, thinking about the debt while feeling a string of emotions, usually worry.

I suggest that you increase your focus on what you do want.

Imagine having the wealth you desire, and feel the way you feel when you already have it.

I love that thought.

If you're not sure what you've been focusing on, look around you.

Whatever has been showing up in your life over time is what you've been focusing your attention on.

Have you been focusing on wealth?

If not, you've been focusing on the lack.

Focus on what you want and you will change your life.

The question you ask today is, How can I continue to focus even more on my increasing wealth?

Today you focus on money flowing towards you, not the money flowing away from you – and then go with the flow.

#62 How to Create Personal Boundaries

You cannot grow without boundaries; however, you can learn how to design, implement and manage boundaries so that the process is effortless for you and for others.

Think of a boundary as a moat around your castle.

That moat was designed to keep the robbers out and the people inside the walls safe to pursue their interests.

During times of conflict, villagers could come inside the castle for protection. A drawbridge spanning the moat provided access to safety, and egress when the coast was clear.

You see some people are needy and they take advantage of others, particularly those who don't know how to raise their own drawbridge – meaning the people who don't know how to say *no* or leave a situation before it starts costing them.

Now a question I often get is, "What do I do when somebody encroaches on my boundaries or exhibits some type of unacceptable behavior towards me?"

And I just think of the castle. The castle dweller would pull up the drawbridge when the bad guys came galloping towards the castle.

This assumes that they had a lookout who would shout a warning in time to draw the bridge. You too must be able to sense when one of your boundaries is in danger ahead of being violated – not as they are being crossed.

You don't start to stop people when they're on the drawbridge; you pull the drawbridge up before they even get there. This sensing is a skill that takes a little bit of time to develop, but you can start right now.

#63 How to Have High Impact Behavior

My life is about making an impact and I ask myself, "What can I do right now in going forward that will have the biggest impact on the results in my business?"

What can I do today to systematize the lead generating part of my business? What can I do to become more referable?

What can I do to bring more value to every person I meet today?

What can I do to make sure that every communication I have makes a profound impact on the lives of others?

I'm turning my action into results.

I love the thought, *I take action.* My strategies and systems create the results that move me beyond fear and quickly into my dreams.

I love the thought that action is my greatest teacher.

My action is my antidote for fear and anxiety and my remedy for indecisiveness.

I love writing down all the things I worry about and then asking, "What can I do to make progress on this right now?" I already feel better.

#64 How to Activate Your Millionaire Self-Image

Imagine a wealthy benefactor offered you $1 million and all you had to do was create a consistent, predictable, reliable business system that generated leads, converted those leads to appointments, turned those appointments into contracts and those contracts into closings. And of course, all the while you were getting referrals and you were building this business and you were controlling your spending.

What would you do if all you had to do was build that, and your benefactor would give you $1 million? Now if you knew that the million dollars would be yours, how motivated would you be to take action to start to make changes in that direction? This wealthy benefactor actually exists. It's you. The reality is you can decide now how much money you wish to create. I call this picture your inner millionaire self-image.

I have studied the lives of Oprah Winfrey, Margaret Thatcher, Estée Lauder, Madonna, Golda Meir and hundreds of other women who have created fame and fortune, and it appears to me that the formula is something like this:

Self-image forms self-esteem, which in term determines our level of confidence. Without confidence, no creativity can occur; no creativity, no material wealth. It takes confidence to go out into the world and break through the financial barriers and beliefs that may have been passed down to you from loving family members. To break through the barriers it may mean breaking the old self-image of the person who comes from lack and scarcity, and replace it with the self-image of the inner millionaire.

#65 How to Be a Manifester

Think of something that you always wanted that you finally got.

Remember the feeling you had before and after you received it; that inner feeling that knew you're going to get it. My friend Thomas Leonard once said to me, "Joe, you can manifest naturally and automatically all the time using your thoughts and your feelings to create what you want." That was 10 years before the book or the movie "The Secret" became mainstream thought.

I looked up the word "manifestation" and here's how I choose to define it: Manifestation is the process of bringing your ideas, concepts, visions and dreams from your inner world into your outer world where you can experience them as real, not imagined.

It's okay to want what you want. The more I coach people, the more I notice that some people have been taught to think that there's something wrong with wanting money, or they've been taught that they don't deserve it, that it's selfish to be greedy. But it isn't selfish to be, do, and have what you want.

When you pursue and achieve what you really want, then you put yourself in a better position to help others do for themselves what they want. So you can let yourself know that it's okay to want what you want and it's okay to have it, too. What would you manifest if you absolutely knew that it's okay to want what you want?

Today you give yourself full permission to manifest whatever you want.

#66 How to Get the Money-Making Mindset to the Right Side of Your Brain Moving Quickly

I heard Chuck Swindoll say that the older you, the more you believe that attitude is more important than facts, and I would have to agree. How about you?

I was looking at the map of the United States and I had this crazy thought – that my brain is like the map of United States. So inside – if I'm standing inside my brain looking out facing south – on the left side is Washington DC with rules, regulations, facts, figures, Wall Street, number-crunching, economies, economists just like the left side of our brain; reasoning, counting, planning, organizing, analyzing.

On the right side is Hollywood, with imagination, stimulation, emotion-packed storytelling, entertainment, fashion, relating, laughing, remembering, feeling.

Then I thought, "Hmm, I seem to analyze with my left side and then agonize over the information in numbers, but then don't decide because it takes the right side of the brain to put it all together so it can form a picture so I can get a feeling that will give me the leap of action." So once the decision has been made, my left side kicks in and wants to get on planning and organizing.

Once you remember that decision-making and risk-taking are right brain functions, you will immediately see the relevance of learning how to think about money with your right brain.

Today the simplest, most powerful thing you can do to possibly increase your increasing wealth and abundance mentally is this: Make it emotional that you become wealthy. Make an emotional decision right now that you become wealthy. Choose to be wealthy because of what is important to you about money.

Once you've made that emotional choice to become wealthy, no matter what, you will begin to take action. Your left brain will start to become aware of opportunities, resources and people that will help you move towards your goal as your right brain feeds it.

#67 Whatever You Focus on Increases

Is it possible in your new world that you have noticed how much everything is constantly changing and how many things are filled with uncertainty?

Companies may be downsizing because of technical efficiencies. Some may be laying off people because of slow sales. Marriages break apart, and someone always seems to be coming up with a better mouse trap.

Everyday I see new ways to get rich. I see new hot ideas. I see people promising that you can become unbelievably fantastically great in only 100 days. Right now we live in an unpredictable, uncertain world surrounded by people who have chosen to run their businesses on personally-get-rich concepts.

In response, I see people who are left feeling with the attitude that they've run the full range of emotions. They feel insecure. They feel shaken. They feel unsure. They're fragile. They're confused. They're angry.

I see people resentful, helpless, hopeless, greedy, guilty and even a bit ashamed.

So what can be done to develop the personal courage? Resolve and resiliency.

To be able to cope with the pressure of life on life's terms, how can we roll with the punches and make better choices with our minds and our behaviors during difficult circumstances?

This is why By Referral Only exists today, because we give you the exact tools and all the training and coaching so you can create a consistent, predictable, reliable monthly income. Using these tools daily will get you out of the mental muck that many lenders and agents find themselves today because they don't have a system to run their business on.

The second way is to develop an attitude of gratitude. Gratitude is a powerful force for wealth creation. Remember, what you focus on increases and when you feel grateful for what you have you focus on the good in your life and it increases. Feel grateful for you financial circumstances whatever they are and they will start to improve.

#68 You Deserve Great Things—How to Become Willing to Receive Them

Life is amazing despite all the pain and the sorrow that it can entail. Life truly is awesome. You are deserving enough of life to have been given that. So anything you might want while you're here is mere trifle in comparison.

The universe gives you all that it gives you without condition. It gives you your life. It gives you breath.

In fact, you could even take the view that the universe has been throwing good stuff to your whole life. The only thing that stopped you from having it is that you have not been willing to receive it until now.

So today tell yourself, "I'm willing to receive all the good that comes to me and accept any thought and feeling that arises."

Today you allow yourself to receive the goodness that you deserve.

#69 How to Use the Power of Affirmation

To get wealthy and to stay that way, you need to become comfortable with wealth. One way you can start conditioning your comfort zone for wealth is to use powerful affirmations. Create an "I am" statement about how you want to be wealthy.

Here's an example: "I am loving the thought that I am fabulously wealthy. I'm loving the thought that I am a millionaire. I'm loving the thought that I'm happy healthy and wealthy."

Say one of these affirmations and notice whatever thought or feeling comes up and then accept it, then added impact, write it down, look in the mirror and say it to yourself daily. Look in the mirror today and say, "I'm loving the thought that I'm fabulously wealthy.

I'm loving my healthy and wealthy attitude.

 I am loving that I am a multi-millionaire." The wealth you desire will come to you faster and faster as you get comfortable with being wealthy now. So what will you say to yourself today? Ask yourself today, "What will I say when I am wealthy and how will I feel when is say it?"

Today you affirm the thought that makes you feel wealthy.

#70 How to Feel How You Feel When You're Wealthy

People move towards what they think about and one of most powerful ways to guide your thoughts is to feel how you feel when you've got what you want.

Stop for a moment and allow yourself to imagine having the wealth that you desire. As you begin to imagine yourself enjoying the benefits of the wealth that you've created, notice what you see and what you hear.

As you allow yourself to do this, feel how you feel when you experience that wealth.

People like what's familiar, and once you start becoming more familiar with feeling wealthy, you unconsciously begin to take steps to bring that wealth into your life. How does it feel to be wealthy?

Today you find the feeling of being wealthy and then deeply feel it.

#71 How to Replace Doubt with Belief

Beliefs shape our reality and our results. Limiting beliefs create limited results. You can find out what your beliefs are simply by writing the word, "Money is..." or "Wealthy people are..." on a piece of paper and then complete the sentence with whatever thought comes to mind.

Now this will start to reveal some unconscious beliefs that you have around money. Once you know what they are, write out a new empowering belief using a powerful affirmation until you really know that *that* is your new empowering belief and you know it's true.

So if you have a belief that lacks any enthusiasm required to create your wealth, you may want to ask yourself, well, what do you really believe? Because without enthusiasm to create wealth, you will create a vacuum for self-doubt.

Experience shows that all natural enthusiasm is based on belief. If you don't have genuine belief about wealth creation, you cannot have genuine enthusiasm.

Of course you're going to have hype, you're going to have a lot of ra-ra, but you don't have genuine enthusiasm in life unless you have something that you truly believe in.

So instead of focusing on questions about money that you can't answer, ask yourself, what are the things that you truly believe? You may believe in only one thing, but what is that one thing?

Right now, you may not know where you're going to get the money to pay a bill, maybe it's for college or maybe just money for the jar for the car. So when you think of money, you may not believe you can do it. What I ask you is *What do you believe in? What are the central things that you really, truly believe at this nanosecond called "now?" What is it that you have no illusions about?*

This is a belief that you can count on.

You believe this. It's a fact. This is bedrock.

You can build your life on this belief. This is what you truly believe, and you would stake your life on this.

Not what your parents believed, not what your spouse or significant other wants you to believe, not what your broker believes, not what your coach believes, it's what you believe in your heart.

What do you really believe is true? I ask myself that question and here are my beliefs:

I really believe in myself. I really believe in what I teach. I really believe I am a loving, generous man. I really believe that I can create my own happiness. I really believe in Olivia and Tracy and the love that I have for them is unconditional. I really believe in By Referral Only. I really believe I'm safe. I really believe everything is in divine order and God is in control.

Once you define what you truly believe, doubt is not nearly the enemy it was.

The future is much brighter than it was because you have a bedrock foundation, a platform upon which to build your future.

So right now, make a list of three to five things that you really, really believe in and watch your doubt disappear.

Today, replace your doubt with what you truly believe. Have a rich day.

#72 How to Create the Jar for the Car

The day my oldest daughter Tracy was born, September 10, 1986, my best friend and mentor Milton Murille said to me, "Today is the day you start the jar for the car." I said, "What do you mean?" He said, "Get a couple of empty five gallon Sparkletts jugs and put them in your closet. Every time you have loose change, throw it in the jar because 16 years from today, you will need to buy that little baby a car. Hopefully, you will have your jars full and they will be the jars for the car." I did what he said, and 16 years later I'd saved $7,200.00 in pennies, nickels, dimes and quarters.

A smart man once said to me, "Joe, when it comes to money most people overestimate what they can achieve in a year and underestimate what they can achieve in five years or 16 years. When you commit to the long-term, amazing things start to happen."

Saving a $1.25 a day doesn't amount to much over a month. But over 16 years, $7,200.00 and it bought, well, half a car. So what sort of life do you want to have in five, 10, 20 years? Go to the website www.ingyournumber.com. That's I-N-G, your, Y-O-U-R, number N-U-M-B-E-R dot com, and discover how much money you need in the future to create a vision of the future that you desire. Then become willing to do whatever it takes to bring that into being.

As you focus each day on the future that you're creating and keep taking action to continue bringing that into being, you'll be amazed at how much money and all the things that you can accomplish as you continue to deepen your money-making mindset.

You may choose to further embrace the wisdom of Woody Allen when he said, "Money is better than poverty, if only for financial reasons."

#73 How to Give More than You Take

I've noticed that people who think financial success comes from resources outside themselves often express their feelings of entitlement to those external sources.

For example, I've noticed, if going unchecked, it's easy to slip into the mindset that our family, our friends, and our past clients owe us their business even if we have not really done anything to earn it.

I have noticed that selfish people never reach their full potential because they're so concerned about what they can get from others that they never think of what they can give.

Now, here's a thought that has worked very successfully for me for over 30 years. "Givers gain and you can't out give me."

All that counts in life is what I have to give and it's a powerfully simple way of developing your whole being. Is it possible that the purpose of your life could simply be to give?

Ask yourself, if your current purpose is generating passion and possibility every day, once you discover that your purpose in your life is to ignite the highest version of your creative self, which I believe is to help people get from where they are to where they want to be, and doing it with passion.

As you may have noticed, it really produces some remarkable results. Do you think it's true that the most powerful purpose is the one that is bigger than you are – which is helping other people?

Imagine having a purpose that is all about what you have to offer the world, not what the world has to offer to you.

Now as long as you are concerned about getting more than you are giving, you will never find and live to your fullest potential, let alone realize the financial abundance that you so richly deserve. Imagine what it will feel like when you love and serve your family, your friends, and your clients in a meaningful way, and you choose to focus only on the money you may make as a by-product of what you freely give.

If you choose only to focus on what you get – and I have done this so I speak from experience – you will never receive what you have the potential to receive, because there is a direct correlation between what we give and what we receive.

So today, ask yourself, how can you get passionate about helping people get what they want rather than getting people to give you what you want?

#74 How to Find Your Security Within

You can choose right now to view your financial security as your personal ability to choose the appropriate response to anything that occurs in your life and your business.

This includes the economy.

Because your security requires creating bankable results like leads, appointments, contracts, closings, and referrals, you can use your skills, your tools, and your courage to produce results on demand.

You choose to understand the truth spoken by Viktor Frankl when he said, "If you have a strong enough 'why,' you can endure any 'how.'" Viktor Frankl was speaking from experience, having survived in Nazi concentration camp. If he can survive that, then you can shine in today's economy, if you have a strong enough "why."

When I ask you what's important about financial security to you, you can reach down into your heart and find your personal drive behind the drive, which triggers the instant search for how you're going to achieve what is really important to you.

You deeply understand that your financial security is solely determined by your attitude, paradigms, and choices.

You find financial security by doing everything imaginable in your power to ensure that you understand and you control as many variables as possible and therefore creating favorable conditions for production.

Because you're financially secure in your skills, your tools, and your learning pace, you live a productive life with the assurance that nothing can ever make you a victim.

You know that being a victim is a choice, not an event, and because you understand the two money-making mindsets – scarcity and abundance.

The scarcity mindset thinks there isn't enough to go around. The abundant mindset says there are plenty of listings, there are plenty of loans, there are plenty of sales circulating and flowing, and more coming in every day.

So stop for a moment and ask yourself, "What evidence can I find today to know that what I need to support my developed security is clearly living inside my current and evolving skills and attitude?"

#75 How to Eliminate All Excuses

Excuses are like a computer virus.

They rob you of motivation, dreams, and your future. Don't let them get away with it.

Excuses typically take the form of "I can't do X because of Y." Or "I would do X, but Y."

But they are not real.

Make a list of all the excuses you've been using to avoid taking action, and then challenge them.

Ask yourself, "How can I do X or what would happen if I could do X?"

Write down the answers and start to take action. As you continue to eliminate excuses and keep taking action, you'll be astonished at your increasing momentum.

What excuses will I challenge today, and in the days and the weeks ahead so I can move towards my financial dreams?

Today, no more excuses.

#76 How to Discover Your Motivation and Your Direction

Some people are motivated by what they want – wealth.

Some people are motivated by what they don't want - poverty.

Some are motivated by both.

As you review the times that you've taken massive action, what triggered your motivation? Was it away from trigger or was it towards trigger or a mixture of both?

If you have an *away from* trigger, imagine what your life will be like in five years if you do nothing about your finances.

If you have a *towards* trigger, imagine what your life will be like in five years if you take consistent action to reach your goals.

If you have a mixture of both, in this case vividly imagine what your life will be like if you choose not to do anything and what your life will be like if you choose to take massive action.

Then, take action.

So what can I do today to spark my motivation?

Today, move *towards* what you want or *away from* what you want, or a mixture of both.

But start moving.

#77 How to Chunk Down, Prioritize, and Get Started Now

Big inspiring goals seem a bit overwhelming at first.

The trick to getting a manageable perspective on a goal is to chunk it down by dividing your goal into five or six sections.

For instance, take a goal like *Achieve financial freedom by 2020.* This might involve different sections.

You might say, *Increase your financial intelligence and then eliminate your debt, and then reduce your expenses.*

Then create passive income, and then create a fund for retirement.

See, once you have all your areas prioritized, keep drilling down until you have a list of action steps so you can start taking action on each one of those sections.

Then get started.

The question you ask today is, "What can I do to make my goal even more manageable so I can take massive action today?"

Today, you chunk things down because it just makes life easier.

#78 How to Shift from Competitive to Cooperative

I imagine you may know someone who over time has developed a scarcity outlook. Maybe they are the type of person who's highly competitive and plays that zero sum game – a game based on one person having to lose so another person can win.

So for example, if they don't get the listing or the sale or the loan, they lose and you win or vice versa. I don't have to tell you how limiting that belief is because you know the opposite belief of competition is, of course, cooperation and interdependence.

Notice that when you bring your consulting and negotiating and organizational skills to a client's problem, you expand the possibilities for everyone in the marketplace.

The skill of pricing the home to sell creates more economy than lack of pricing skills. The ability to help a seller understand that his or her home has no intrinsic value, that it's only worth what another person's willing to pay for it, creates opportunity for everyone. You may ask yourself, "How is that, Joe?" Well, the home that is priced to sell creates opportunity for the lenders, for buyers, title companies, escrow companies, and about 15 other industries. The house that does not sell only sucks the resources from everyone in the community.

After 30 plus years of coaching, experience has shown me that the most successful, most fulfilled, happy agents and lenders have extremely optimistic views of themselves in the world and they have the consulting, negotiating, and organizational skills to match.

"When I win, everyone wins." It's even easier to develop an optimistic outlook based on a win-win than you might expect.

#79 How to Access Your Abundant Mindset

The first step in overcoming the scarcity mindset is to consciously recognize and accept the abundant nature of the universe and all your potential as a By Referral Only consultant.

As you know, there are more than enough people who are buying, selling, and borrowing in the universe to support your abundance.

You can consciously choose right now to view life abundantly, to think and act abundantly, and to love and serve others without fear of loss. So how do you do that?

Well, it's easy.

Open your consciousness to your unlimited resources by asking "how" questions. If you say, "I can't find anyone to list their home with me." You will prove yourself to be right.

But when you ask, "How can I find a seller today who wants to sell their home with me today?" Your mind starts to search for a possible solution.

If you say, "I can't find a loan for the client." You move into something that is very scarce. You might say, "How can I find a loan today for this client?"

Your abundant mindset starts to generate possibilities. Watch what happens when you imagine yourself using "how" questions in all your situations where you used to say "I can't." Today, reach for your abundance and have a rich day.

I suggest today that you ask "how" questions that can create the leads, the appointments, the contracts, the closings, and the referrals that allow you to be financially free.

#80 How to Plug the Money Holes before You Make More Money

It's a fact. People who experience more of what they desire in life are the people who do not back away from money problems or difficult financial tasks, because they have plugged up all the holes in their financial bathtub.

Now you may ask, "Joe, what does that mean?" Well, imagine your current money situation is like a bathtub. I wonder, is it possible that you may have a few holes in your tub? If that's true, it's best to plug them up before you increase the flow of water. It's a little bit like saying that the holes are wasteful spending habits and expensive financial obligations that you are not really committed to, and because of the holes, you create a mess in your life no matter how much money you pour into it.

Imagine you've plugged these holes by eliminating waste and developing healthy spending habits. Then you can increase the flow, secure in the knowledge that your increasing wealth and abundance will stay in the tub. So the faster you clean up your money mess, the faster you can make more money. I caution you, if you just choose to make more money without patching the holes, it just gets messier. I've heard it said that the more money that you make, the more it tends to amplify those emotions and those unhealthy behaviors that accompany them. So what's the solution? First, plug the holes with new financial responsible behavior. Second, you can choose to get into a more positive state of mind.

Become a money-making monster because the healthy ones are willing to budget their money, their time and energy, and protect their time only for projects that stimulate their money-making mindset. The money-making mindset makes people invest wisely and turn a sharp focused eye towards what most keenly concerns them – their positive emotions.

#81 What Would Happen If You Could?

What would happen if you could see yourself as you really are? The you that is happy, fulfilled, and free may have been asleep. What would happen if you believe that everyone who creates wealth has experienced setbacks along the way, and that most people give up when they meet a setback and an obstacle? Most successful people, like you, do what you did when you learned to walk. You fell and got back up.

When you fall over, you learn from the experience. You pick yourself up and you keep going. What would happen if you could let go of any financial fear and lack and any feeling of not good enough? What would happen if you did believe that you are good enough right now? What would happen if you could describe yourself as already perfect?

So you don't need to change yourself right now. It may take some time to create the wealth that you desire, but when you stay true to yourself and you keep learning, you develop the wisdom and the insight.

What would happen if you could see that your dreams of the "you" you'd like to be are in your current reality – just somewhere in the future?

You already are the perfect person. It's time to wake up to that reality of who you really are. Focus on your "you" you know is true, your true nature. Imagine that. Love yourself back to reality and awaken from the dream.

What would happen if you knew you could not fail, that failure is an illusion that it is only possible to fail if you set a limit for yourself?

It may take some time to create the wealth that you desire. When you stay true to yourself and you keep learning and you develop the wisdom and the insight, anything is possible. You might even decide right now to eliminate failure from your vocabulary. Imagine that.

What would happen to your life if you could enjoy learning from your setbacks that you have experienced in the past?

#82 How to Use Your Ideals to Set Direction and Measure Progress, Not Perfection

Ideals are like the horizon.

As you move towards them, they move further away. They're great for setting a direction but terrible for measuring your progress.

Why?

Because when you reach them, you'll discover new ideals. People who are successful and happy measure their progress by looking back at how far they've come.

The miserable ones look at their ideals and feel downhearted because they haven't arrived yet.

The truly successful approach is to look at how fare you've come and feel good.

Then look at your ideals and feel excited about how much you can keep enjoying the journey.

So the question I ask you today is how far have you come in your wealth journey?

Today you focus on your progress, not your perfection.

#83 How to Be Happy and Wealthy

People think I'll be happy when – but our minds like what's familiar, so if you want to be happy when you're wealthy, practice being happy now.

The more you enjoy the process of becoming wealthy, the more you'll enjoy the result. Laugh, celebrate your achievements, share your success with friends and loved ones.

Experience shows that when you commit to being happy now, the journey to your increasing wealth becomes much more enjoyable.

You might even like to imagine how you'll feel when you're wealthy. Then start feeling that right now. It doesn't cost any extra to feel good. So what else can you do right now to increase your happiness today and into the future?

I'm suggesting that you seek happiness and wealth today.

#84 How to Be Present

What I'm discovering when helping people narrow their focus is that most problems can be solved by focusing on what is the most important use of their time and their energy right now to produce the most significant results.

The first thing that I've become very aware of is that before you can create a future, you must resolve the past and perfect the present.

Many of us are driven to create fabulous futures for ourselves, or to spend a lifetime in our quest to resolve the issues that effect and limit us, while there's nothing wrong with either of those approaches, yet there's a weakness in them.

And the weakness is that neither is about the present moment.

And both are about different time zones, the past and the future.

And it's worthwhile to go into the past and to visualize the future, but only with both feet really firmly planted in the present.

My mentor Thomas Leonard used to say "if you want to create a fabulous future, make the present, the right now, absolutely remarkable."

So what is the present?

The present is simply today.

The reality of your life, today. What's *so* right now?

#85 Focus on Opening Yourself to Being Present While Others Are Speaking

I open myself to focus on being fully present while others are speaking. This is not a communication trick or a technique. This is how you access your authentic power, by deeply listening to the *words* but more importantly, the *feelings* behind the words.

One of my coaches has helped me listen better when she taught me to *patiently*, and lovingly, and respectfully listen with respect, even when the other person is saying something that is complete nonsense. She calls it "with a curious heart." Open yourself to being present.

Open yourself to being present every time someone speaks. Listen with a curious heart.

 That's really worth practicing today, asking, "Am I listening right now with a truly curious heart? Am I present right now?"

You'll find your authentic power lies in that moment.

#86 How to Emulate an Iceberg

Imagine this. The foundation upon which we create our lives can be compared to the shape of an iceberg. Imagine an iceberg that is drifting across the ocean. The portion of the iceberg that is above the surface is maybe 20% to 15% of the total iceberg. Then 80% to 85% to 90% of it is *below* the surface. Although the part that is visible may look very tiny, the part below the surface is spectacularly huge. The larger portion *beneath* the surface is what gives stability to what is *above* the surface.

I believe that as we choose to create great things in our lives, it might be worthwhile emulating the iceberg.

As we create what we want, what can we learn from the shape of an iceberg? On your notepad or in your journal, if you could just doodle out an iceberg. Could you learn about stability? Could you learn about persistence and predictability and consistency?

Instead of the whole form of the iceberg being exposed above the surface of the ocean, the *biggest* portion, the largest section, lies *deep* beneath the water. The iceberg displaces the water, then generates an upward buoyancy that forces the iceberg to float. Now, is it possible – just imagine – is it possible that this may be a model for productivity?

Every single person has a surface self; that's what others see. Then we have an inner self that is not visible to other people.

Consider this. When your inner self is larger than your surface self, you seem to possess a core confidence.

Experience shows that people with core confidence have profound inner depth; a radiant, powerful, refined light – a Martin Luther King light. Profound depth.

Confidence is dependent on the extent of a person's foundation. The part that remains deep, deep below the surface. What I've learned from this natural wonder of an iceberg is my sense of stability, predictability, consistency gives ways to confidence.

Think of a person that you know who is a master; a person who radiates a light of core confidence. Think of the person that is closest to you that you admire most, that when you think of core depth, core confidence, rock-solid, deep core confidence, who comes to mind first?

I'm talking about the kind of confidence that no matter what kind of trouble they're confronted with, they have the *depth* to deal with it and always stay afloat.

#87 Defining Your Single Greatest Strength

What do you do best? Because that is where you get your most predictability from.

I have these moments where I feel uncertain and insecure and a sense of uncertainty. Whether it is at a professional level or a personal level, the one thing that I always do is go back to where I know my greatest strength is.

My greatest strength is in learning and teaching and emptying myself so I can give to others.

I was at a conference in Los Angeles and there was an exercise in the conference where the speaker said, "Turn around and share with a person." And I was sitting in the very back row and a person turned around and looked at me and said, "Here is my problem." I could definitely tell she was lacking confidence and security.

And I was a little out of place, too. I felt my insecurity and my uncertainty also, and I knew that the easiest way for me to get my confidence was to be in the role that I love to fill which is to guide and to teach and to just give all that I could give; all of my expertise.

The exercise was done in about 15 minutes and this person that was in front of me goes, "Oh my god I feel like I am so grateful I sat in front of you. I got more from this 15 minutes than I have gotten from the whole conference." And in that moment I felt so confident.

Give what you give away naturally to others professionally and for fun and watch how confident you will get in yourself. #88
How to Define Your Priorities

What three promises could I make and keep in the next 90 days that would make a 50% difference in whatever by the end of the year?

That is such a great question. Whenever I am feeling uncertain and unsure, really wondering what is going to happen next personally and professionally I will take out my journal and I will say okay what three promises could I keep in the next 90 days? I think, I just want to work on it this season. What three promises in this season could I make and keep that will make a 50% difference in my life by the end of the year?

It could be a physical life, it could be a financial life, it could be your family life, it could be your friends, it could be finances, and it could be faith.

Pick three areas of life, and look for three promises that you could make in the next 90 days in each, and watch what happens.

As soon as you get some clarity you will start to get your confidence back.

#89 Keep a Positive Progress List with You at All Times

Always ask yourself whenever you're feeling uncertain "What are the top 10 accomplishments in my life?"

"What are the biggest things that I have achieved?"

"What are the things that I can always look back at and see and know that I got that accomplished?"

And when I look back and I see my accomplishments – especially when I write them down – I look at them and I feel more confident and I say, "Boy if I can do that, I can do anything."

So I look at what are the accomplishments I really feel good about, and I make a list of those, and I instantly get my confidence back.

So if you are lacking that confidence, I imagine most of you are confident 99 percent of the time, but that 1 percent of the time…

Make a list of the things that you have accomplished in the past and watch how quickly you gain your confidence back.

#90 How to Create Core Confidence

From my past 25+ years and thousands of one-on-one sessions it's obvious to me that you either have the core confidence to go out and create what you want or you're wearing a mask – trying to be someone better than who you believe you really are.

Core confidence is a result of two things:

(This is just my experience. See if it fits for you.)

Number one: Core confidence comes from having unconditional love at the *core* of your life.

My research and study and insight tell me that if we get this core, we get it before we enter school. So between the ages of birth and five years, you got a *core* sense that no matter what happens, no matter what mistake you make, you will always be loved.

This *foundation* gives you incredible confidence. If you grew up with a mother and a father, brothers and sisters, who without any condition, completely saturated you in love, you can go out into the world and make mistakes because it doesn't matter; you're loved at your *core*.

Now, there are those of us who grew up where love was conditional or inconsistent, maybe dysfunctional. Maybe it was abusive families, or alcoholic families, or broken families. Only you know personally, at a personal level, what happened between zero and five.

What I know is when I'm coaching, I usually love to just explore that a little bit with you. I say, "Tell me a little bit about what happened early, early in your life; the day you were born to the time you had to go public." We go public when we go to school.

What I listen for is what was the upbringing? If the upbringing introduced us to inconsistent, conditional love, I know it affects our ability to focus. I know it affects our ability to have core confidence. I know it affects our ability to believe in optimism. It creates self-doubt.

Now here's the good news. Eighty percent of the people who are reading this right now grew up with inconsistent, conditional love.

The fortunate 20% are people like Sir Richard Branson – read his autobiography, where he grew up with his extraordinary mother and father who just lavished him in love and unconditional...beautiful. He's willing to go out and take extraordinary risks because it doesn't matter. He can't fail. He's at his core, he's loved.

People come to me and ask about themselves, "Why do I procrastinate? Why do I sabotage my success? Why do I not follow through?" I like those questions. I think they're valuable, but I'm not sure it's what we really want to explore together.

Do we really want to dive into your childhood and look at the lack of love that you received before you went to school and as a result, you're just recreating that pattern over again, this takes enormous courage. Are you willing to let go of the patterns you discover ? If so take a deep dive into you past and do the work that will set you free.

#91 How to Learn to Teach

Prosperity, abundance, wealth, freedom, money – whatever form that you are looking for as an outcome is the by-product of doing what you love.

Look inside your business right now and ask, *How much do I love my business?*

Because your business will create problems for you. It is difficult.

I love this thought about life and business.

Business is a series of problems, disciplines, rituals, language, and tools, all designed to solve problems. That is what your business is.

Now the question I ask you is, "Do you love your business, loving what you do, loving what you are learning?"

Because that is really what you do as an entrepreneur.

You are learning, and growing, and expanding, and you are finding people to teach that to. Your business is an impersonal system that creates prosperity and abundance for you.

What business will do is create problems.

That is what business does.

I am challenged with my business a lot, but it is okay because I love to learn. And I learn to teach. And if you really love learning, and growing, and expanding, and finding new insight and new awareness, and then whoever crosses your path in life, whoever you come in contact with – that is who you teach.

That is who you share your insight and your awareness with. And then you build a business over here to make money.

The business is going to have problems. Business is difficult. It is full of pain. It is full of joy. It is handling complex problems.

Problems in your business call forth courage and confidence, wisdom and awareness. Problems often bring out the courage in you. Without problems we won't grow. We won't grow mentally. We won't grow spiritually.

Wise people like you and me come to embrace problems.

Weaker people are trying to create freedom from problems. They are trying to create a pain-free business which actually ends up creating lots of anxiety.

You see, what I know about problems in business is they demand growth from us. Carl Young says, "You do not solve a problem – you simply out grow it."

Problems give us an opportunity to recommit to our business. If you have a problem, it is not about getting rid of it, it is about committing to growing as a result of that problem.

And I love that notion.

I love the notion that all my problems are lessons that God really wants me to learn. And when I learn a lesson, then I can teach it to whoever is ready to learn it.

#92 How to Express Your Unique Gift

Powerfully productive people have discovered that around them, things get done.

There is a moment in time when you realize at a very deep level that you are going to improve your life. And one of the fastest ways to improve your life is to create massive value for others.

When you make that choice you now ask yourself, "Who is the one person who will fully support and enable the purpose of me giving myself fully to creating value for others?"

Then detach yourself from all the stuff that "must get done" so you can focus on keeping your promise. Trust the person you have chosen to support you to take care of the stuff and the outcomes.

To get to the place that you are not attached to the outcome all you ask is, "How can I serve?"

When you get to that point that all you want to do is serve, then you owe it to the people that you want to serve to have all the support you need.

It is important to understand that when you choose to allow yourself to be weighed down in activities that are not your unique ability, you are denying an opportunity to a person who is actually more qualified than you are to do that work.

And when that person does that work, it frees you up to really help more people that only you can help. They are helping you in their unique way so that you can help others in your unique way.

In my business, writing this book is my unique gift. Everything that must happen to get this book to you – someone can do better than me.

I owe it to you to get the best people to support me to keep my promises. That is how I have become peacefully, powerfully productive. And you can do it, too

#93 How to Slow Your Brain Down

I am going to use an analogy of the engine of an automobile to give you a context on how to manage your time.

Now the analogy I am going to use I am just making up. So I am going to suggest that the engine revolves at a certain number of revolutions per minute, or RPMs.

So let's call 100 revolutions per minute the optimum speed (when the engine is operating smoothly and efficiently at a speed that it won't burn out).

Now I am also going to correlate that with the velocity of your mind. So if you can imagine that the optimum speed of your thinking is 100 revolutions per minute.

At 100 revolutions per minute you can think all day long without any stress. And you can function. Your mind works well. You have adequate profundity. You have the ability to pay attention with little or no distraction. You have the capacity to concentrate.

You can clear your mind easily. You can say, "I am going to do a quick sit down and just take out my journal and I am just going to get everything out of my mind onto paper."

And you can do that quickly and efficiently. You are enjoying your experience. You are a person who feels calm and you experience deeper feelings of joy and happiness and you don't need a lot of vacations.

You can go on vacations but you don't really need a lot of vacations because you don't really feel a lot of stress. You are operating at a speed in your mind that is optimum and is natural and it feels good.

Distracted Zone – 100 to 200 RPMs

Now if you were to speed your mind up from 100 to 200 revolutions per minute, I call this the distraction zone.

In the distraction zone we have a tendency to have attention deficiency. You know what that is like.

You forget your car keys.

Then you run upstairs and a moment later go, "What am I up here looking for?" You are distracted a lot. And you don't have a lot of control over your attention. Mentally it is very inefficient.

It is not that you are a bad worker. You are just a person who doesn't have really great focus. And you duplicate a lot of your effort. And there are a lot of things that you do over again.

The attention is more on your thought than really being in the present. It is like driving a car at 200 RPMs, going super-fast.

You are forced to focus on the road ahead and anything that would distract you could cause catastrophic injury. It is easy to make mistakes when you are revolving at 200 revolutions per minute. You would think that would be better for your business to focus, but in fact, when your mind is moving fast enough to pay attention or something bad could happen, you are in the distraction zone.

For people who are in the distraction zone, boredom becomes something that they absolutely cannot tolerate, because boredom means they are not being nurtured by the moment. They are addicted to the speed.

In my experience, when I am really revved up into that 200, 220 range or my mind is moving really quickly, my partner will say something like, "You are here but your mind isn't. You said you weren't working, but you are thinking about work." You have to practice detoxing. You might have to watch TV to calm your brain down.

They say men have to go into their cave and just disconnect so they can slow everything down. That is because it is revolving at such a high speed and in order for them to shift from work to home you must slow the mind down. I'm not sure it matters if it's a man or woman, the same thing happens.

I have also noticed that people who are constantly running up in the 200 range spend a lot of money on stimulation. And they hate standing in lines. They hate anything that requires a level of patience.

Have you ever seen a snow globe, where you shake the glass ball and all the snow starts to move and then it starts to calm down?

That is the person who is operating at 200 RPMs. They are constantly shaking. There is this storm going on in their mind and in order to calm down it has to be still. And when it gets still it starts to get clear.

Hectic and Scattered Zone – 200 to 400 RPMs

There is a level even higher than distracted. Let's call it between 201 to 400 RPM's. It is the scattered and hectic range. You know when you are with a person like this. They are very jittery. They are restless. They are not capable of attention in general.

They are capable of attention only during an emergency. But as soon as the emergency is over they are back to their jittery ways.

They have tons of activity going on around them and hardly get anything done.

But, boy, it looks like there is stuff flying around everywhere.

I have watched people who are in this state of scattered hecticness come in to my life and they are just all over the place.

That whole myth around multi-tasking was designed for the person who operates between 200 and 400, where it is a super over-active mind.

So they can text and drive while having a cup of coffee and talking to the person next to them.

None of those things are being done well because they are in the hectic scattered zone.

Unbalanced – 800 RPMs

And there are of course higher levels of being mentally sped up. Let's say all the way up around 800, double the last level.

That is completely unbalanced. That person is a candidate for a nervous breakdown. There are severe mental dysfunctions.

I was just at Starbucks earlier today and there was a lady sitting out front. She is homeless and may be off her meds; I don't know her whole story but I can make it up. Just say looking at this woman that she is in that unbalanced zone and her mind is just moving so fast, so rapidly that she has absolutely no control over it.

And whatever is on her mind is just coming off the tips of her lips. Just speaking and screaming and yelling. There might be a hundred different voices inside that head just all talking at a very rapid rate.

If you have a propensity towards negative thinking, the faster your brain goes the more likely you are to experience levels of depression.

And if you are a more positive thinker the faster your mind goes the more likely you are to experience distraction.

I have had moments where I got really depressed and felt a lot of despair, and what I noticed was that I was trying to think and do too many things. But my thought process was negative at the same time and I got really down.

Especially when you get insecure; when you feel insecure in your relationship with your buyer, your seller, your power, or your space, your partner, your spouse, what happens is the brain starts to speed up. You start over-focusing, getting intense.

One of the easiest ways to kill a relationship is get insecure. Your insecurities usually bring the worst out in everybody. I know that when I am insecure I bring the worst out in my clients, in my partners, and my relationships. And when you are insecure, what happens is the other person feels that insecurity and it just brings the worst out.

So just notice that insecurity starts to happen when you start to think and create in your mind a whole story about something that is not really happening. But in your mind it is happening and it is happening very fast.

80 to 99 RPMs – The Productivity Zone

Now why am I sharing this with you? What does this all have to do with productivity?

Well have you ever had a day where you said to yourself, "Boy that day really went by fast? I just wish I could get more time." The fact is we can't get more time, but we can slow time down.

The way we slow time down is, of course, only an illusion. We slow time by slowing our thoughts.

So imagine taking your revolutions per minute down to the between 99 and 80. Imagine that. And I would call that range the optimal, super mental power.

You get ideas that will surprise you.

You tap into genius and levels of observation and awareness that could never happen at the level 100; but now you have instant access to when you are dropping down into that 80 range.

You will also notice your habitual thinking.

You will notice at 80 the habitual thoughts that you have; those reoccurring thoughts.

So imagine you have a deal that is falling out of escrow right now. You're in 200 RPMs. There it is again; you're always thinking about it. You are in the swamp of thinking about it. You can't think yourself out of the problem, and the more you think about it the deeper you get into the problem.

When you slow it down and you take it down to 80 what you start to notice is, "Oh, my gosh, I am inside the habit of thinking about this deal.

"It is not really me.

"It is quite impersonal as a matter of fact. Nobody is doing anything to me. It is a deal that is falling apart and there are a lot of elements to it."

And at 80 you can become more impersonal to the things that are occurring around you.

At 200 everything is personal.

I know I can get more done in a calm hour than I could get done in a week of hectic-ness or a couple days of distraction or even a day at 100. I can get done in an hour at 80 so much more, and the quality of what I can get done is so much more.

40 RPMs – Nirvana

Now there is even another level below 80, and let's call that "Nirvana." That level goes all the way down to 40.

Slow it way down. Nirvana is the place where wisdom in its most profound experience is occurring.

And life is in slow motion. And you can actually see the life force. Remember the movie, *The Matrix*?

The digital screen and all the numbers represented the life force and the code of life. As Neo became more attuned with his wisdom, the code would slow down so that he could see it— could see the code underneath the "reality." But he could only do that by slowing down to about 40 RPMs.

How to Slow It Down

I want to share with you what I do to slow it down. There are three things:

Number 1: I find whatever reoccurring habitual thought that is coming up. Whatever seems to be most present for me, what I do is I make it impersonal. As soon as I make it impersonal, instantly I drop down into a lower speed.

I know that when I go into meditation I can make it impersonal so I can say to myself, "Anything that I am feeling right now is part of the human condition.

"I am not alone in this.

"This is the way the human condition operates. It is not personal to me. It is impersonal. This emotion I am experiencing is not exclusive to me. Why would I think I would be above that? How arrogant that would be of me to think that I would be above not feeling this. And who knows what is going on at a higher level or bigger level. What are all the other parts to this?"

What I know is God has a plan and I have a plan. And I know that God's plans work and mine don't. It is probably best for me to disengage from my plan and get above it and look at the bigger picture. And as soon as I do that I slow down.

Number 2: I move right into forgiveness. And forgiveness is just a beautiful frequency that helps you slow down. And forgiveness is allowing everything the way it is occurring to be okay with the way that it is occurring.

What I mean by that is I go inside and I look at anything that I feel any angst about.

Number 3: I find gratitude. I say, "I am so grateful for the time that they *did* invest in our community. I am so grateful for the money they *did* invest in our community. I am so grateful for all that occurred *while* they were here." And this process takes about 15 minutes for me. So I will sit and I will watch my thoughts come up, and any of the habitual ones are the ones that God has given me to work on.

I love Carlos Castaneda, where in his books he talks about the hero's journey. Carlos Castaneda comes to Don Juan and says, "I have this person in my life that is causing all this trouble for me. I can't believe it. They are just causing me all this disappointment."

And Don Juan goes, "Yeah, way to go! Cool man, that is great! You have a tyrant in your life. You have a tyrant! That is so great because that is the person who gives you a chance to find God. Without this person you wouldn't find God. They have been given to you to bring you to your spiritual awareness."

I look at that and I go, "Wow that is cool." So it becomes impersonal, and then right into forgiveness, and I forgive you. Then right into "I am grateful." And in fifteen minutes I can go from 200 revolutions down to 50 or 40 revolutions per minute. And then from there, from that place I make my choice to bring *myself* to my work. I make a choice to bring myself to this book.

I would encourage you that if you could find that place each day, there are such extraordinary aids available to assist you.

Aids to Slowing Down the Mind

Meditation is an incredible aid. Anything that brings you joy – if it is gardening, walking on the beach, exercising – anything that would bring you joy helps you slow things down.

Time management at the level that we are speaking today is slowing down the velocity of your mind so you can have a higher quality of thought, which allows you to get more significant work done in a shorter period of time.

So just in review we are suggesting that 80 to 99 revolutions per minute is where you're calm, having a deep feeling of joy and happiness without any stress.

As soon as you take it up higher than that and get into that 200 area, you start to look for stimulation, you can't stand boredom but you find yourself duplicating your effort.

You are losing your keys, can't remember, have attention deficit. And if you take it up even faster than that, you get really scattered. You get a little jittery. Be careful of pouring coffee on a brain that is operating at 400. It could throw it into the imbalanced zone and there is where you make dangerously difficult and lasting decisions that often you regret for a life time. It is best only to make important decisions at 100 or below.

So, if you are in the midst right now of making a life-changing decision, make sure you are making it from the wisest part of you. Not the intellectual fast mind.

Then drop it down. Dropping it down into the super mental power area below 100 and even lower, to where life is in slow motion into that 70 to 40 range.

#94 What Is Your Unconscious Commitment about Building a Referral Business?

What is your truth about your commitment to creating referable relationships?

Do you really want to have healthy genuine relationships to be the foundation of your business?

You have a choice. You can be transactional.

You can help a person buy sell or borrow and never have a genuine referable relationship. You can attract people through advertising and marketing and never really get too close to them and certainly never let them get to close to you.

You can do the deal and move on. You can play on the surface and have little or no depth to your relationship.

You can easily attract people who have the same level of commitment. You can easily find buyers, sellers and borrowers who see you as a means to an end.

They don't want relationship, they want a good deal and they don't really care about you and your personal being.

I would know.

For my first 10 years in business, I was not conscious about who I had to be and the quality of commitment that was required to have genuine committed referable relationships.

Here is my bottom line truth about how I began the process of creating a conscious referral business – I never had the slightest chance of creating and sustaining a referral business until I made a conscious commitment to creating healthy, happy relationships in my life.

Up until the moment I made a conscious commitment to attracting and keeping great healthy clients, my unconscious programming was running my life and business.

A truer statement was my unconscious commitment was doing a better job of *ruining* it than running it.

Looking back over my life, I can see now that the biggest and hardest decision I made was to change my unconscious programming about attracting genuine healthy referable relationships.

Through lots of personal development and reflective awareness, I have come to the place where I believe that whatever is going on in my life is what I am committed to either consciously, unconsciously or both.

The power of commitment has given me everything I have in my life now.

If you want to know what you're committed to, simply look at the results you have in your life.

#95 What Are the Ten Internal Conflicts You Must Overcome to Attain Referral Mastery?

Are you the type of real estate or mortgage consultant who knows you should be asking for referrals, but you are not?

Try this. Out of these 10 questions, how many do you answer yes?

1. Have you developed the habit of forgetting to ask for referrals?

2. When you are with people do you spend all your time talking about current business and do you not leave enough time to ask for referrals?

3. Do you feel awkward or uncomfortable when you ask for a referral and they don't know anyone?

4. Do you feel that asking for a referral is a sign of weakness and believe that if they know anyone they will refer you without you having to ask?

5. Do you ever feel that asking for a referral is unprofessional?

6. Have you ever felt like you were begging or groveling for business when you are asking for referrals?

7. Have you had a bad experience asking for a referral in the past and you have decided not to do it anymore in the future?

8. Are you uncomfortable with the scripts or dialogues you have been taught to use to ask for referrals or have you not had any training in asking for referrals or both?

9. Do you ever feel you don't deserve referrals?

10. Do you feel that most people have had a bad experience referring a friend to a typical salesperson so you don't bother asking?

So let's call the 10 questions "your internal conflict."

You must have all the systems and processes in place so you really believe you provide extraordinary value.

You must have a core belief that says, "What I offer to my clients in the way of my consulting, negotiating and overseeing of all the details of the real estate and mortgage transaction is so much more valuable than any other agent or lender could ever imagine providing.

The person you ask for a referral must also believe that your value and expertise is far superior to any other option.

This is the big secret.

You must be able to communicate clearly that the people they care about will never know about you if they choose to not refer you.

#96 How to Use the Referral Continuum

Here are examples of ten possible introductory referrals you may receive. The first one has the least potential for a successful conclusion and the last has the most potential.

When you receive a referral learn to rate them on a scale of 1 to 10, using this continuum.

1. Your client says, "I think the guy down the street is moving. You should call him. I don't know his name, but I think he is moving."

2. Your client says, "If I know of anyone, I will give him your card and ask him to call you. It is really up to him if he wants to call you".

3. Your client says, "Here is a list of all the people in my neighborhood; you can send out an endorsement letter from me – if you write it I will sign it."

4. Your client says, "Here is a list of all my friends with their phone numbers. If you send out a change of address card to all of my friends you might get some new business that way."

5. Your client says, "I am having a company Christmas party and I would like to invite you. At the party I will tell all my friends that I am one of your clients"

6. Your client says, "There are three guys at my office who said they will be moving. If you give me your cards, I will pass them on and encourage them to call you."

7. Your client says, "There are three guys at my office who said they will be moving; if you come by the office today I would be glad to introduce you."

8. Your client says, "If you ever need me to call anyone for you and let them know how great you are, just call me and give me their number and I will call them right away for you."

9. Your client says, "My friend Andy is moving. I told him all about you and he is expecting your phone call. Here is his phone number."

10. Your client calls you and says, "My friend Andy is on the other line he wants to buy a home. He is highly quailed and he knows you work By Referral Only and he wants to buy a house this week."

#97 How to Stop Needing Referrals

On a recent coaching call one of my client's said, "I really need to get more referrals."

My response was, "As long as you need them, you won't get them".

She asked me to explain what I meant.

The more you need something, the more you attract the energy of needing.

Have you ever heard this, "Whatever you focus on you attract?"

Try this…

Right now, begin to stop needing referrals.

When you need something, it means you don't *have*.

When you come from a place called "I need" you're in scarcity and lack.

From that place, you attract to you neediness.

When you think and say I need more referrals – what you manifest is a need for more referrals.

That is a rather simple goal to achieve – you end up needing referrals and you have achieved your goal.

Starting Today You Choose To Be Referable vs. You Need Referrals

Affirm these two statements out loud with passion and commitment:

I love the thought of being a highly referable consultant who easily receives two great referral leads from each of my current clients.

I love the thought that today I have decided to get two great referral leads from each of the people I talk to in my center of influence.

What you think about, you talk about and what you talk about, you bring about.

The paradox of referrability is that you choose who will refer you vs. you need people to refer you.

When you need referrals from someone you begin psychologically and emotionally leaning on people.

Stuart Wilde introduced the concept of leaning to me in his wonderful little book, Silent Power.

For now keep playing these words in your head:

I love the thought of getting two referrals from my current clients or from any one I speak to in my center of influence.

GO FOR IT!

#98 How to Create the Referral Mindset

Remember that when you put yourself into a referral mindset, you feel good about the process of asking for and getting referrals.

The sooner you get your head in the right place, the sooner you will become referable.

Work on each of these seven concepts to develop the referral mindset. Once you have fully assimilated these seven, you are 80% of your way to being By Referral Only.

Realize that the primary purpose of your business is referral.

Empower yourself to only work with people who want to work with you.

Focus on the power referral dialogues and stop hoping for referrals.

Establish a powerful set of boundaries and communicate them clearly.

Resolve to make no more excuses believe that everyone knows someone.

Run your business as if what other think about you makes absolutely no difference.

Advise your clients without ever compromising your integrity.

Love to serve with an open heart – even when your client's heart is closed.

About Joe Stumpf

Joe Stumpf has been in and around the real estate coaching and training business since 1977.

In 1981, he started his training and coaching company, which has grown to be one of the largest coaching companies in North America.

Joe Stumpf has a subscription-based company with over 5,000 clients, the purpose of which is to teach the principles, provide the tools and systems, to be highly profitable and at the same time serve others with the heart of a "Super Servant".

Joe Stumpf invests most of his time and energy in creating, writing, and video/audio recording, while his leadership team runs his company's day-to-day operations.

His work has been a wonderful vehicle to express his creativity, as through it he gets to live a life fully expressed as a model of possibility.

It is the perfect forum for him to discover and allow his most authentic self to be publicly shared.

In all of Joe Stumpf's work his intention is to create the next version of himself, one which is more aligned with his soul-purpose.

He has gained a sense of mastery on the goal line while maintaining a sense of sacred purpose.

Reading, writing, teaching, and coaching is woven into his fabric.

He possesses a beautiful coaching gift of being able to channel insight and awareness to people when they seek clarity and direction in business and life.

He helps people in profound ways so they can experience the shifts they desire as a result of crossing his path.

He views this as his life's purpose.

You're welcome to take a closer look at Joe's work at MyByreferralOnly.com or you can write to Joe at JoeStumpf@gmail.com.

35313540R00090

Made in the USA
Lexington, KY
06 September 2014